# THROWING
# BONES

## Crystals, Stones, and Curios

# THROWING BONES

## Crystals, Stones, and Curios

INCLUDES 20 UNIQUE CASTING BOARDS
FOR DIVINATION AND INSIGHT

MYSTIC DYLAN

WEISER BOOKS

This edition first published in 2024 by Weiser Books,
an imprint of
Red Wheel/Weiser, LLC
With offices at:
65 Parker Street, Suite 7
Newburyport, MA 01950
*www.redwheelweiser.com*

ISBN: 978-1-57863-836-9
EISBN: 978-1-63341-340-5

Cover and interior design by Karin Skånberg
Cover and interior photographs by Nicki Dowey
Board and cover illustrations by Kuo Kang Chen

Other pictures courtesy of Bailey Burton/Unsplash;
Alberto Menendez Cervero/Shutterstock.com; Eli
Defaria/Unsplash; Mallory Johndrow/Unsplash; Luca
Volpe/Unsplash

Printed in China by 1010 Printing International Ltd.
10 9 8 7 6 5 4 3 2 1

When sourcing bones and material for your rituals and
readings, please remember to be respectful of others,
protect nature, buy ethically sourced goods, and not
cause harm to animals or your environment.

# CONTENTS

## CHAPTER ONE
## CLEROMANCY
## (THE ART OF CASTING LOTS)
*page 22*

## CHAPTER TWO
## NECROMANCY
*page 40*

# CHAPTER THREE
## SCRYING
*page 44*

# CHAPTER FOUR
## PENDULUMS
*page 52*

# CHAPTER FIVE
## OTHER FORMS OF DIVINATION
*page 56*

# CHAPTER SIX
## BOARDS
*page 76*

# Meet Mystic Dylan

For over two decades, Dylan has studied and perfected his craft in the occult. At the early age of nine, Dylan and his mother frequented a local occult shop in Los Angeles, California, where his attraction to witchcraft would pave the way to his career in life. He mastered palmistry and tarot, honing his skills on friends and family before officially pursuing a formal education across Los Angeles, New York, and New Orleans. His natural connection to mysticism fueled his ongoing study and exploration of the arts of witchcraft, voodoo, conjuration, and shamanism. Now a fully practicing, professional witch, Dylan uses the Craft to assist both friends and clients in their personal lives.

Born from Cuban, Irish, German, and Native American bloodlines, Dylan attributes his spiritual gifts to his many ancestors who walk and work beside him, guiding him on his sacred journey. He has worked for over a decade as an independent scholar, and as a film and academic consultant. Dylan currently lives and works in Los Angeles, where he teaches classes, runs his own coven, co-hosts the podcast "Life's A Witch," co-owns the III Crows Crossroads online store, and is the co-founder of the brick and mortar shop, The Olde World Emporium.

IG: @mysticdylanofficial   Theoldeworldemporium.com

# INTRODUCTION

Have you ever rolled dice or used marbles? Played a game of chance or dominoes? How about flipping a coin to ask a yes/no question? Now, imagine if all these systems could also be utilized to delve deeper into your psyche and help you peer into the future, take a look at your past, and address issues in your present.

The art of cleromancy is often attributed to witches because of its strong link to spirit work and its direct ties to magic and ancient pagan divinatory practices. In fact, one could argue that cleromancy, along with scrying and necromancy (which this book also explores), is the divination system most strongly linked with witchcraft and magic. The use of cleromancy has appeared in several movies and TV shows in this context, including *Pirates of the Caribbean, American Horror Story: Coven*, and *The Chilling Adventures of Sabrina*.

Within these pages you will first be introduced to the art of cleromancy/throwing bones—or as I like to call this reading system, casting fortunes. It is one of the oldest divination systems that is still used to this day, and different forms of cleromancy are found all over the world. It is through casting fortunes that you can truly enhance your intuition and connect to the spiritual, earthly, and supernatural realms. Through collecting your totems, trinkets, and "bones" (as I like to call them), you are building a unique alphabet and language that allows you to answer some of the most important questions one may have to ask.

Later in the book you will also be introduced to other popular forms of divination—including scrying, pendulum dowsing, astrology, and rune craft—so you can find the method that best suits you.

This book is unique in that it not only walks you through these divination methods and offers you step-by-step instructions on how to begin reading, but it also contains boards that will act as placemats to further enhance your readings—just lay the book flat and cast directly onto the page.

Remember that while learning cleromancy, scrying, and necromancy will awaken your psychic gifts and offer a truly enchanting way to give readings, the real magic and insight comes from you. Learn these sacred arts, but also remember to rely on your own intuition.

# WHAT IS DIVINATION?

People have been attempting to peer into the future for centuries
through various different methods.

Today, the most common form of divination that sticks out in everyone's mind is the standard pack of tarot cards. One might also think of a crystal ball, a popular image found in cartoons and shows depicting psychics and fortune tellers. However, these are merely two of the various other forms of divination that exist throughout the world. Divination is the practice or art of gaining prophecy, spiritual insight, divine wisdom, or predicting the future through various tools or rituals. The word "divination" derives from the Latin *divinare*, meaning to foresee, foretell, predict, or to prophesy.

Tarot cards

Crystal ball

Divination in its many forms can be found in most spiritual and religious circles, and is even mentioned several times in the Bible, specifically the Old Testament. In fact, you will even find mention of bone throwing and cleromancy (also known as casting lots) several times in the Bible, once in the book of Joshua, where God asks him to cast lots to determine how to divide the different parts of Judaea (Joshua 18:5–6), and once more when the art of casting lots is described as a way to receive wisdom directly from God: "The lot is cast into the lap, but its every decision is from the Lord" (Proverbs 16:33). The practice of cleromancy is used once more in the New Testament, when the remaining 11 disciples of Jesus cast lots to find a proper replacement for Judas (Acts 1:123–126).

Aside from casting lots, the Bible also references other sorts of divination, such as dream interpretation and scrying in a goblet or cup, both of which were skills that Joseph had, as well as reading animal entrails and watching omens in nature. As can be seen from the Bible, the original forms of divination were used to consult a deity or supernatural being. The diviner or seer proceeding over the divination acted as an oracle or medium, thus interpreting and relaying what the divine intended to be said within the divination session. This divination session was done with the use of tools such as bones, runes, fire, and oil lamps.

Despite its usage in the Bible and acceptance in the early church, under the Christian Roman emperors divination became strictly associated with witchcraft, magic, and paganism. At around the same time, in the 4th century CE, Augustine of Hippo, also known as St. Augustine (354–430 CE), similarly decreed that all forms divination and anything linked to the old Roman religion was sorcery and therefore illegal. This decree influenced the views of both church and state, ultimately affecting the entire Roman Empire and Christian orthodox.

Through divination we can not only peer into the future and see potential outcomes, but also connect with

spirits and gain wisdom and information from the divine. Divination is more than just a form of fortune telling; in fact the two, while similar, are very different. Fortune telling is mostly for pure entertainment and amusement, with no real goal other than to predict forthcoming events, very similar to a Zoltar machine you'd find in a carnival or the Magic 8 ball you've probably shaken at some point in your youth. Divination is deeper, more ritualistic, and usually requires a belief in fate or some sense of spirituality.

Today, divination is just as popular as it was centuries ago, with tarot and oracle decks being widely available in most book and novelty stores, as well as stores such as Target and Walmart. Divination allows us to connect with the energies surrounding us and check in with other vibrations, as well as foresee any possible shifts and obstacles that may head our way. The reading of runes, a magical alphabet system from Norse and Germanic regions, is also a popular divinatory practice used today.

Divination has been utilized through many elaborate tools, but also through common ones such as eggs, smoke, ink, and water, and the use of casting lots and bones, which we will discuss in much more detail later on. Divination allows us to put the puzzle pieces together, solve the mystery, and look at the bigger picture.

In the following pages you will be introduced to a variety of different divination systems. Which ones appeal to you? Some are very obscure, while others are quite simple. You do not have to try all of them, but you may wish to explore your options and see what appeals to you. I firmly believe that everyone has the gift of intuition, but some may be more attuned than others, and that's okay. Not all divination systems will appeal to you, or be easy to learn. I easily memorized the 78 cards of tarot, learned palmistry, and gravitated toward bone throwing, but have no connection with or ability to retain the knowledge of runes like my dear friend Chad, nor can I learn astrology as well as my friend Becca.

When it comes to divination, I say, to each their own. Hopefully you'll learn to explore and connect well enough with the forms of divination presented here to give truly magical readings.

Modern rune stones

# TYPES OF DIVINATION

There is not just one standard form of divination. In fact, there are hundreds of different divinatory methods that have been practiced around the world.

Some are done with common household items such as reading tea leaves or a candle flame, or are easily recognizable to us—for instance, using a spirit board or pendulum. Other methods are more obscure and outdated, such as reading the entrails of an animal or the migratory patterns of birds. Many of the same methods of divination were used by different people and cultures, but had different names, styles, or functions.

Most divination techniques require the reader to interpret different patterns, or to pay attention to the system and base the answers on what it is the reader seeks and feels.

This list mentions several different forms of divination that, while obscure at first, are known methods through which the reader can tap into the universe, gain spiritual insight, and unlock information on a situation. Which of these methods calls to you? This is by no means a complete list; rather, it focuses on the divinatory methods one could practice fairly easily or utilize with this book and the methods provided herein. The divination methods that are taught and referenced in this book have an asterisk (✳) next to them.

# DIVINATION METHODS

**Abacomancy:** to read the patterns of dust, dirt, sand, or the ashes of the dead.

**Aeromancy:** to read cloud formations, weather conditions, and wind patterns.

**Apantomancy:** interpreting chance encounters with animals.

∗**Astragalomancy**: the throwing and reading of dice or knuckle bones (see page 58).

∗**Astrology/astromancy:** to read the celestial bodies and stars (see pages 62–69).

**Augury:** interpreting the omens found within the behavior of birds.

**Bibliomancy:** interpreting and reading random verses or words in a book.

∗**Cartomancy:** the reading of playing cards or tarot (see pages 72–75).

∗**Cleromancy:** the casting of stones, bones, curio, and the reading of lots (see pages 22–39).

∗**Dowsing:** the use of twigs, rods, or pendulums to find water, lost objects, or to communicate with spirits (see page 54).

**Ifá:** generated with palm nuts, opele, cowrie shells, etc.

∗**Necromancy:** communication with the dead (see pages 40–43).

**Numerology:** utilizing numbers for prophetic insight.

∗**Oomancy:** reading eggs, both yolks and shells (see page 60).

**Pyromancy:** reading images in flames and fire.

**Rumpology:** interpreting the impression and shape of the buttocks.

∗**Rune craft:** the utilization of runes for divination (see page 70).

∗**Scrying:** gazing into mediums (such as reflective surfaces) to see future events and gain prophetic insight (see pages 44–51).

**Tarotmancy:** the utilization of tarot as a main divination purpose.

**Tasseography:** reading with tea leaves and interpreting their patterns.

# UNDERSTANDING PSYCHIC SENSES

Ever get a gut feeling in your stomach right before something big happens? Perhaps you've had a dream of a scenario that actually played out in real life. Maybe you've heard messages or voices from something that wasn't there. These are all things that occur when we are connected to our psychic senses. Everyone has psychic abilities and intuition. Some are inherently stronger than others, but when we strengthen them, we create a deeper psychic connection that, when paired with divination systems such as cleromancy, can add a tremendously strong layer to readings.

Our psychic senses are divided into different categories. I like to call them "the clairs." Knowing about and learning how to work with the clairs allows you to build a deeper connection to the world around you on a deeper spiritual level. The clairs are essentially the psychic senses of the physical senses we already work with innately. As long as you take time to focus on these skills you will be able to learn and use them to their full potential. Everyone has these skills to some extent, but some might be stronger and more proficient in certain areas than others. Regardless, all psychic senses need to be exercised to allow you to have a better control of your readings and strengthen your connection to the spiritual realm. Here are the main psychic senses and techniques to help you harness them. Which one do you find you connect better with? Which one are you having a harder timer with? Remember–practice and patience are key.

## Clairvoyance

This is the psychic ability to see into the realm beyond. Clairvoyance allows you to see the spiritual world with what is known by many as your third eye, perceiving images that you never would have seen in the real, mundane world. Through clairvoyance you receive images, colors, and visions that do not always make sense, often requiring analysis and interpretation. This is one of the more frequently used and well-known spiritual senses because of its overuse in pop culture and depictions in film and TV.

Clairvoyance is usually easy to interpret and to understand, making it another popular choice for those learning to strengthen and develop their psychic skills, because most people are already very used to interpreting things with their eyes. When we see something in our spiritual vision, we often are able to literally see it in our mind's eye. Seeing something with your third eye looks a lot like recalling a memory in your head; how clear it is depends on how connected we are to the person or scenario we're receiving the image about. This is a very good skill to strengthen and get a hang of if you are a visual person, since it will greatly improve how you perform readings.

*Techniques to enhance clairvoyance*

**1.** Meditation is always a very good idea when trying to learn any type of divination or spiritual technique or skill. It allows you to really focus upon it and unlock secrets gradually through your own growing spiritual understanding. One should always give meditation a try to improve psychic abilities.

**2.** Visualization will help you to better enhance visions and the certain shapes they construct in your mind's eye. This will also allow your third eye to be more open to seeing things, which will greatly increase your clairvoyance because you are using your third eye more. Look up visualization techniques online or listen to guided meditations and let your imagination run wild.

**3.** Pay attention to any images that enter your mind. Write them down, look them up, and try to interpret them.

**4.** Try to use zener cards in order to improve your viewing skills.

**5.** Look at images in clouds, trees, nature, etc.

**6.** Ask a question and then close your eyes to see the answer in your mind's eye.

## Clairaudience

This psychic ability to hear the spiritual world through your spiritual mind or ears allows you to perceive noises, sounds, and other audio stimuli from the spiritual planes of existence, including voices, spiritual audio cues, and maybe even energy itself if you become proficient enough in it. Clairaudience is great for people who need to hear things in order to gain insight. Experiencing clairaudience sounds a lot like hearing disembodied noises with no discernible source, like when you hear someone call your name but don't know which direction it came from. If you can learn to trust what you are hearing, you can develop a great connection with the spirits and energies that are around you, and the spiritual world in general.

*Techniques to enhance clairaudience*
1. Meditation.
2. Develop your spiritual awareness of low, usually unperceived sounds by going to an open spot in nature such as a park, allowing your mind to go blank, and listening to your surroundings.
3. Learn to connect with music by listening closely to your favorite songs and feeling the energy and emotions behind them.
4. Imagine sounds happening in your head; this allows your clairaudience to get used to trying to hear sounds that are not there.

## Clairsentience

This is the psychic ability to feel information and be able to read it just from the feelings that you are getting, without any other stimuli tipping you off to that information. Clairsentience is a pretty hard one to explain but it is very different from the other clairs and psychic senses, because in this practice you are feeling the energy of a person and getting no other information, no other signs; you just know it. This is a way to clearly sense the people around you. Often those with these gifts have a harder time putting down clear boundaries with friends and loved ones because they know when someone is withholding, or will feel things before they happen.

*Things that will help you learn and experience your clairsentience*
1. Meditation.
2. Learn to trust your gut so that you can learn how to differentiate between information that you create versus the information that comes to you via your perception.
3. Be aware of your thoughts, since some of these could be the higher realms communicating with you.
4. Look at pictures of people and try to tell everything about them just by looking at them. Do not judge them, but allow your intuition to come out.
5. Think about something and see if any information comes up about it randomly.

## Clairescence

Also known as clairscent, clairalience, and clairolfaction, clairescence is the psychic ability to gain information and prophetic insight via smell. Clairescence is one of the odder senses, and one that you don't hear too much about. This is your ability to spiritually smell, and it's about perceiving odors and fragrances that do not have any known source in your surroundings. This is a very interesting way to get insight from your perception via smells you associate with other constructs or information. This process is not done with your physical nose but you will still smell in the exact same way. Through the interaction of these smells you will gain insight into the information that is around you.

*Techniques to strengthen clairescence*
1. Meditation.
2. Try to imagine smells appearing in your vicinity that are not there.
3. Smell things and see if you can get information on that thing that you shouldn't be able to. Pretty much what I'm saying is, go out and smell things!
4. Pay attention to any smells that come into your perception so that you can analyze them.

### Clairtangency

Also known as psychometry, clairtangency is the psychic ability to touch. This not only allows us to feel spiritual energy with our hands, but also to read into the information that energy holds simply by touching it. By touching something, you can gain so much insight into the construct that you are making contact with. Once you get good enough at clairtangency you won't even have to touch the physical object in order to get insight into its energies; all you would have to do is feel the energies around it. Clairtangency can be done with any part of your body, but is primarily done with your hands, because of the very sensitive hand chakras that reside within your palms. Being able to feel the energy around you with a spiritual touch can help you in many ways in your craft.

*Things that will help you learn and experience your clairtangency*
1. Meditation.
2. Pass your hand over objects and see if you can get a sense of where they have been, or the energies that they produce.
3. Go to a museum. Do not touch the exhibits, but raise your palm up to them so that you can feel their energies. Name off some items or information and then check the description to see if you're correct.

### Clairgustance

This is the psychic ability to gain prophetic insight via taste. Clairgustance is another one that is kind of out there for most people. This is the ability to spiritually taste things, even if they do not reside in your physical mouth. If you know how you will be able to taste things energetically, you will be able to gain insight into the energies that you are tasting.

*Techniques to help you strengthen your clairgustance*
1. Meditation.
2. I know this sounds weird, but in your mind try to taste people's energy to see if you can tell the difference in their flavors, essence, and substance.
3. Whenever you taste something, try to actually focus in on what that taste is, in order to get used to the sense of taste.

### Clairempathy

Also known simply as empathy, clairempathy is the psychic ability to sense and feel emotion. Empathy will allow you to feel other people's emotions and gain insight into them and the world around you. Empathy is a very powerful connection that, if used correctly and with a lot of understanding, can make interacting with all things a lot better. With empathy, you are able to pick up on everything that an entity may be feeling. It is a very deep personal insight that allows you to experience things from another's perspective, at least in an emotional sense.

*Things that will help you learn and experience your clairempathy*
1. Meditation.
2. Sit quietly and try to feel your own emotions so that you can understand how emotions feel to you and interact with you.
3. Try to feel into the emotions of the people around you and see if you can get any worthwhile results.

# TRADITIONS AND TECHNIQUES

Throwing bones has been practiced for centuries by peoples all over the world.

Some divination practices are specific to certain religions and spiritual faiths, such as Ifá, which is not only a system of divination, but also a spiritual practice usually regulated to practitioners of Santería or other Yoruba religions. While for the most part divination of any method is open for all to practice, it is important to know the origins and spiritual or religious background and associations tied to any form of divination.

Cleromancy, specifically bone-casting (which is also known as bone throwing), has a scattered history, since it has been practiced in varied forms by different cultures. The form of bone throwing that is described and used in this book is part of the folk magic and divination system made popular in the American South by practitioners of hoodoo, rootwork, and conjure. This type of bone divination has deep roots in South Africa, especially amongst the seers, diviners, and healers of the Zulu tradition.

During the Transatlantic slave trade, African folk tradition was immersed and mingled with European superstition and sorcery, giving birth to a unique blend of magic in the Caribbean and North America that made bone throwing the perfect divinatory technique for root workers, witch doctors, Obeah practitioners and witches alike.

It is very important to know that there is no one way to throw or cast bones for divination. Also, in regards to cultural appropriation, it is very important to understand that while the origins and method of bone throwing might have been formulated by a certain group of people, bone throwing is not a closed practice or restricted to any one person. It is not tied to any one religion and can be practiced by anyone regardless of race, gender, or creed. Methods of bone throwing and cleromancy vary drastically between individuals.

When it comes to traditions, every bone reader is different. This system is usually taught by someone who learned from a family member or a reader, who in turn learned from family or a family tradition. I've met a reader who uses only chicken bones and gives different parts of the bones specific meanings, such as the wishbone for luck and wing bone for travel, while the feet indicate a need to cleanse or break away from a situation. Another reader and dear friend, Mike, utilizes Norse runes in his cleromancy

kit. You can also paint, mark, and decorate your own bones—another dear friend, Kristy, stained and carved her bones from ribs she had for dinner one night. She also made me a beautiful set that I always use.

How you build your bone and curio divination is up to you. Some folks read with only a certain or single type of bone, from one specific animal, such as a chicken. Some only use bones from animals and won't mix in any other curio or household items, while others use everything but bones. Building your cleromancy set is personal. Feel free to incorporate crystals, charms, beads, shells, or dice with your bones, as some sangomas do, but no matter what natural and artificial curios you include in your kit, the practice is still called "throwing the bones."

Where and how to perform readings is just as personal. Some traditionalists and old timers perform readings by casting their bones on the ground or at the feet of the person they are reading for. This method is used to this day in Africa. Others will cast their bones on a special cloth they prepare themselves, or on the hide or pelt of an animal. At the back of this book you'll find some wonderful boards that you can easily cast on to help enhance your readings.

When not in use, you may want to keep your bones in a basket or box on your altar, or keep them by your nightstand. Here are a few tips and tricks to help get you started and better enhance your readings.

* Every bone/curio in your kit is personal and picked by you! You don't need to have a specific bone in your kit just because you read it here or it's traditional. (I have no spiritual attachment to armadillos, insects, or arachnids, for example, so none of that symbology will ever go in my kit.) If there's something on the list of bones/curios that you don't connect with, don't put it in your kit.

* Once you give a bone/curio a specific meaning, that meaning should remain and not be changed.

* Anything can be a bone/curio in your arsenal, as long as it can be thrown, isn't too big, and has meaning and value in your readings.

* Try to avoid giving too many bones/curio the same meanings and associations. You don't need four bones to represent protection, or six bones representing change. This will only confuse you and lead to a very vague reading.

* Try to limit the number of bones that are the same in your arsenal. For example, I had three alligator feet in my kit for a long time, and while they had different meanings, I eventually just ended up using one and have found it much more effective.

* Pay attention to the position of the bones, their distance from each other, and which direction they face.

* Always remember to interpret the bones/curio in accordance with the question that was asked, or the intention behind the reading.

* Don't forget to use your intuition, paying attention to the signs and symbols you see.

* Take your time and breathe.

* Use a pointer, such as a stick or bone, that is utilized just for pointing out bones to the person you are reading for.

* Always remain objective and refrain from sugar coating your readings.

* If you do use multiples of the same bones, pay attention to their patterns and how close they land to each other.

* If not using a grid, give specific meanings to the directions in which the bones land (closer to the querent (the person who is asking the questions) indicates present, farther away is future. Left side is mundane and family, right side is career and money, etc.)

* Cleanse your bones/curio frequently or between readings with incense smoke, salt, etc., to remove any negative energies they may have absorbed during readings (see pages 36–37).

* Thank your bones/curios, spirits, ancestors, or higher powers for their energy and wisdom after readings.

* Your reading style and system will always be different from others.

* Let your style of reading reflect your personal faith, understanding, and connection to spirit and symbolism.

CHAPTER ONE

# CLEROMANCY (THE ART OF CASTING LOTS)

Today, when we think of fortune telling or divination and the tools used therein, we think of tarot cards, crystal balls, pendulums, and maybe runes. However, prior to the mass publication of tarot in the 19th century and the New Age boom in the 20th century, most tools used for divination were makeshift tools conjured up by the readers themselves.

The seers, conjurers, and mystics of yore did not have metaphysical stores or the magic of the worldwide web. There were no retailers for crystal balls, pendulums, or scrying mirrors. Instead, they used what was accessible to them: bones, shells, nuts, and roots foraged in nature; broken pieces of porcelain; pebbles; or a key found around the home. These odds and ends were collected and then strewn out over a cloth or mat and intuitively gazed at, until all the pieces formed an answer or answers to a question. This is known as cleromancy or casting lots.

The practice of cleromancy is one of the oldest forms of divination, if not the oldest. Because it was so widely used in the ancient world, it is hard to pinpoint exactly when and where it was first utilized. The casting of lots for decision-making and divination can be found in ancient Egyptian texts dating back to 1279 BCE. The Ancient Roman poet Virgil (70–19 BCE) mentions the Greeks and Romans using lots for divination and prophecy in several of his works.

Casting lots for divinatory and prophetic purposes was not a structured practice that was fixed throughout the many regions of its use. In Greece, lots were thrown or cast and consisted of tiles or bits of pottery marked with the Ancient Greek alphabet, similar to Nordic runes. Practitioners also used knucklebones from cattle, sheep, or goats. In Rome, lots were drawn from a basin or jar and were often read individually, with each token or bone representing an answer, name, or decision.

The ancient practice of casting lots was also seen as a way of channeling deities and spirits. The connection between casting lots and the divine was so strong that it was even mentioned in the Bible (Joshua 7:14–18 and Samuel 14:37). The casting of lots to determine God's will was a popular practice amongst many early Christians throughout the Roman Empire. In the East, casting or drawing lots was the primary form of divination, especially in Taoism in China and omikuji in Japan.

Today's methods of casting lots for divinatory purposes come from Africa, such as the Yoruba-inspired form of cleromancy called Ifá, as well as Obi and Diloggún.

These methods of divination originated in West Africa and found popularity amongst the New World lineage of the Yoruba religions such as Santería, that was birthed at the time of the Transatlantic slave trade. In South Africa, the Zulu Sangoma diviners and seers used large bones and other natural curios such as roots, stones, and shells in their cleromancy sets, which many modern Hoodoo practitioners in the American South use today.

The mingling of African traditions with Indigenous Native American and European folk beliefs, customs, and superstitions gave birth to a whole new form of divination practices, as well as making cleromancy and casting lots ever more popular in places such as Europe, the Caribbean, and North America.

Today, cleromancy is often referred to as "bone throwing" due to the historical and popular use of bones in the practice, but the "bones" do not have to be actual bones—they can be natural curios or personal objects you've collected and wish to add to your cleromancy set. I personally like to call this practice "casting fortunes," as I feel it offers those who may be unfamiliar with the practice a gist of what to expected from a reading. Unlike tarot, which requires study and memorization, all cleromancy calls for is a belief in spirit, trust in your intuition, and a familiarity with the items and curios you collect for your personal kit. Once you've established a link with your "bones" and have given them meaning and properties, you're ready to cast fortunes and do readings for yourself or others.

# BUILDING YOUR PSYCHIC ARSENAL

In days of yore, cultivating bones for divination and magic was not an easy task. It usually required foraging through woods and rough terrain for dead animals, or a visit to a butcher or hunter. Today, one does not need to go to such lengths to acquire bones to build a reading kit.

When we think of bones, we picture animal or human skeletal remains. However, when using the word "bones" for cleromancy, we are referring to all items that are cultivated for your "bone throwing kit." While the majority of the items will be natural, such as bones, shells, roots, and crystals, they also can include other baubles and trinkets such as dice, coins, keys, or even a porcelain doll arm. (Yep, that's a popular item for bone throwing kits.)

While there are documentations of what commonly goes into a bone throwing kit, it is important to remember that the art of bone throwing is a folk practice that varies from practitioner to practitioner, and especially from region to region. Creating your own bone throwing kit allows you to build a connection with the bones you wish to include in your arsenal and create a definitive divination system based around your personal practice.

To begin cultivating and building your kit, it is important to know what you wish the kit to reveal and answer for other people as well as for yourself. Think of the questions you'd ask during a reading, or what you've heard asked by others. Will your readings answer questions about love, money, the future? What about those wishing to speak to spirits or know about their spirit guides? After you navigate the questions you want your readings to answer, think about the bones and baubles you wish to add to your kit. What are your favorite animals? How about a favorite crystal or color?

Bones can be sourced from all over. They can be found at oddity shops and occult stores, foraged while out hiking and, of course, purchased online. When searching for bones, think of the intention and what you're looking for. What will the bone represent? The majority of bones procured by oddity and occult stores are ethically sourced, but if you have any reservations, don't be afraid to ask. As you collect your bones, you should cleanse and consecrate them to remove their previous energy and debris, and then give them their magical and oracular purpose (see pages 36–37). Cleanse them by sprinkling the bones with salt and water, smoking them through incense, and holding them in your hands. You can then consecrate them by either naming each bone or giving it its function, for example: "This snake vertebrae bone will represent change and transformation." The bones can then be added to your cleromancy kit.

Remember, bone throwing is personal and different for every reader; you and you alone will dictate what a bone means. However, once you state the function of a bone it should stay with that function. You are building a fixed system that you can follow. If you're afraid of forgetting what function you've given the bone, write it down. A bone throwing kit usually consists of a mat on which one throws the bones, a shell, bowl, or box within which the bones reside and are thrown from, and a pouch or larger box to transport the bones. Most readers keep their kits in a bag or small box.

Aside from the items you'll be adding to your kit to read with, you should also consider having items at your disposal to help not only set the mood, but also enhance your reading and offer spiritual and psychic protection. A candle and small shell or dish for water may be included to attract spirits, salt could be sprinkled around the area for protection, or a herbal bundle could be burned. Displaying a black crystal or stone, such as obsidian or jet, can offer protection from malefic entities and can be used to banish bad vibrations. Think of anything that you'd wish to have with you during a reading to set the stage and enhance your practice.

## THE OBJECTS

Below are examples of bones, curios, and baubles from my bone throwing kit that are common in other kits, which you can use as examples of what to look for to create your own kit. Some of the meanings for the bones are common practice and universal, so you may see some crossover—for example, using rib bones for protection, since rib bones protect the organs. Think about the function of the bones and the animal archetypes as you build your arsenal.

### Bones
**Ankle bone:** Flexibility/Endurance
**Foot:** Travel/Stability
**Ribs:** Protection/Withholding
**Teeth:** Communication/Gossip
**Vertebrae:** Strength/Burden

### Crystals
**Amethyst:** Psychic insight/Rest/Meditation
**Bloodstone:** Ancestors/Past relatives
**Carnelian:** Health/Living blood relatives
**Citrine:** Money/Career
**Smokey Quartz:** Spirits/Outside influences

### Curios
**Coin:** Money/Prosperity/Yes or No questions
**Dice:** Used for timing/dates or answers regarding numbers
**Key:** Answer to a question/Solve a problem
**Nuts:** Birth of something new/Creativity
**Roots:** Stability/Ancestry/Lineage
**Seashells:** Feminine/Emotions/Fertility

A cleromancy kit might comprise bones only, or it might be a mix of items you have gathered that already have meaning for you—or to which you ascribe a meaning.

# BUILDING YOUR CLEROMANCY KIT

Building a casting kit is a fun and spiritual experience for a reader. Each kit is unique, because each reader gravitates to different tools and is attracted to different items that they want to have in their arsenal. It is important to know when building a kit that you cannot have too much or too little in your kit. However, you may want to start small and expand as you grow in practice. I myself have collected a handful of "bones" (I use this word as an umbrella term for all items in my cleromancy kit) that I will swap out from time to time.

It is also important to remember that while we may only want items in our kit with positive meanings and intentions, life is not perfect and comes with obstacles, so some of your bones will have to represent the darker and harsher aspects of life, such as a thorn representing pain or hurt. Make sure that each "bone" in your kit has a specific meaning that you will remember.

Over the next few pages you will find a list of objects that are often found in in cleromancy kits and their correspondences. You are not required to obtain and use every item on this list or use their meanings. This is only a guideline. Only you will know what item is best to have in your kit, and what it means to you.

Listen to the bones: they will speak to you. You also may find that certain items that are not on the list jump out at you, which may be a spirit calling you to use it in your kit. Give it a purpose and add it in.

When looking through the list of items, you will find that many of them share the same correspondences and meanings, so don't be afraid to add different meanings that you connect with. Remember, too, that you only need a few items from each category. Your kit does not require every crystal or bone from the list. That's what makes cleromancy so unique, because the items you choose for your kit will be totally different from everyone else's.

# Roots, spices, nuts, herbs

**Adam and Eve root:** love, a couple, partnership
**Black bean:** family, protection
**Black peppercorn:** revenge, unwanted visitor, enemy
**Buckeye:** could represent a man, business, finance, or luck
**Clove:** love, money, friendship
**Devil's shoestring:** general good luck, gambling, winning a court case
**High John the Conqueror root:** love, protection, strength, success, personal strength, money
**Nutmeg:** love, luck
**Toadstool:** spirits, fairies, the supernatural
**Tonka beans:** money, fertility

# Stones, minerals, crystals

**Agate:** health, emotions (lighter shades), money, finance, physical (darker shades)
**Amber:** protection, wealth, inheritance
**Amethyst:** psychic connection, intuition, healing, addiction, spirituality
**Apache tears:** sign of grief, needing to heal, comfort
**Aventurine:** luck, wealth, career
**Flint:** ancestor work, protection
**Gold:** prosperity, wealth, masculine energy
**Hematite:** Healing, grounding, protection
**Jade:** healing, health
**Jasper:** protection
**Lapis lazuli:** divine work, spirituality, spiritual healing, magic
**Malachite:** wealth, health
**Moonstone:** feminine power, lunar energy, sorcery
**Obsidian:** protection, grounding
**Pearl:** love, passion, prosperity
**Pyrite:** money, career
**Quartz:** healing, cleansing, needing to clear
**Rose quartz:** love, romance
**Tiger's eye:** courage, strength, willpower
**Turquoise:** ancestral magic, earth, balance

## Common household items, random curio

**Chain**: constraint, obstacle, toxicity

**Coffin nail**: supernatural, ill intent, malice, significance of a curse

**Coin**: prosperity, wealth

**Cowrie shell**: represents a female, female energy, yes answer

**Crucifix**: spirituality, faith, protection

**Dice**: used to indicate length of time or a specific amount, answer to a yes/no question (odd means no, even means yes)

**Key**: opportunity or obstacle (depending on the direction), opening doors, seeking answers

**Magnet**: attraction, energy pull or suck

**Marble**: healing, mental health

**Pin**: obstacle, challenge, pressure

**Red brick fragment**: home, family

**Ring**: promise, contract, union

## Animal bones and curio

**Alligator**: strength, determination, protection, stubbornness

**Badger**: defense, fortitude, survival

**Bull bones**: fertility, virility, strength, pride, ego, masculine energy

**Cat**: spirituality, luck, independence, curiosity

**Chicken**: cleansing, clutter, indication of being spelled (depending on direction)

**Cow**: domestic life, kindness, nurturance

**Coyote**: trickery, wit, humor, sexual infidelity

**Deer**: nature, love, new romance

**Dog**: loyalty, faithfulness, obedience

**Fox**: cunning, intelligence, diplomacy

**Goat**: sex, sexuality, pride, wilderness, passion

**Human**: ancestral, spirit work, the dead, spirit allies

**Rabbit**: haste, timing, timidity, fear

**Raccoon**: dexterity, cleanliness, cleverness, theft

**Raven**: messages from the dead, transformation, prophecy

**Snake**: stealth, cunning, renewal, sexuality, secrecy

**Wolf**: spirit guidance, path finding, pact, promise, intuition, leadership

# Bone meanings and symbolism

**Ankle bones:** mobility, goals, journey
**Arm bone:** work, labor, assistance
**Backbone/vertebra:** courage, backbone, resolution
**Baculum/penis bone:** male sexuality, virility, dominance, luck in gambling
**Claws/talons:** defense, cleansing, protection, attack
**Femur/thigh/leg/shank bones:** travel, race, endurance, leverage, movement
**Finger/knucklebone:** dexterity, connection, physical touch
**Foot/hoof/paw:** grounding, completion, security, stability
**Jaw/mandible:** speech, gossip, discourse
**Pelvis/pubis/hip:** fertility, sexuality, weight-bearing
**Rib bone:** protection, concealing feelings and emotions
**Shoulder blade:** burden, responsibilities
**Skull/cranium:** mind, essence, thought, knowledge
**Teeth:** biting through, attack, defense, secrecy, lies, deceit, argument
**Wing bones:** flight, movement, travel
**Wishbone:** wishes answered, hope, dreams come true, yes
**Wrist/hand bone:** dexterity, flexibility

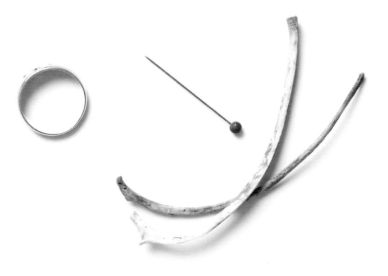

# HALF IN/HALF OUT:
# MAINTAINING SPIRITUAL BALANCE

As you progress in the art of cleromancy and casting fortunes you will learn to trust your intuition and make a deeper connection with the spirit realm. Casting fortunes is a unique divination system because it allows you to not only tap into the spiritual realm, but also to form a spiritual connection to the tools you utilize during your readings.

The majority of the items in your kit will be natural and of the earth. Bones have a psychic connection to the animal they come from and thereby have an essence attached to them. Nuts, roots, and crystals all contain a natural essence and spirit. Any additional curios you might have added to your kit (such as coins, keys, dice, etc.) will have a previous energy attached to them that is often linked to the previous owner or place of residence, or they will share a psychic link with you from when you set their intentions and made them part of your reading arsenal.

While being open spiritually and trusting your intuition is a key part of doing readings and casting fortunes, one must also be grounded in reality as well. This is what I like to call "being half in/half out." This means that while you should allow your intuition to flow freely during a reading and make connections with spirits and nature, you should also be firmly rooted in the mundane world and not let your imagination or spirituality get the best of you. This balance is achieved by having a healthy dose of skepticism and knowing the boundaries of psychic work, spirituality, and what magic can truly achieve. I often refer to myself as "the skeptic psychic." I know my limitations, and I know what can be perceived or achieved during a "psychic reading."

When performing a reading, we have to listen to our inner voice, trust our gut and senses, and look at the omens displayed in the tools we use. However, we must not let these things dictate our life, and we mustn't go overboard. When you make connections with spirits, make sure you establish boundaries and dictate when and where you will interact with them. I've seen many a client or colleague who seem to be ruled by their connections to spirits and deities; they are always spiritually open, and therefore vulnerable to psychic attacks and being spiritually drained. This often leads to personal instability that can affect your day-to-day life and mental health.

Spiritual balance is extremely important if you're to have any success casting fortunes or performing any other type of divination or psychic work. You must be able to not only compartmentalize your intuition from reality, but also not let your ego get the best of you. Sometimes readers feel they need to prove to their client or the person they're reading for that they're the real deal, causing them to make things up, or add additional information for flourish. Getting performative in a reading does not legitimize your skills, but actually makes the reading feel like a hoax. Take your time, look at all the items tossed out before you, go over each one and their meaning, and their partnerships with each other. If you don't feel the presence of spirit or hear anything, that's totally fine. I oftentimes am more academic in my reading style, especially when it comes to cards, since it's a fixed system. Also remember that while cleromancy is a great tool for connecting and speaking to spirits, it is not a necessity and you can always read the fortunes as is, without any input or connection to spirits.

# PREPARING FOR A CLEROMANCY READING

Cleromancy is one of my favorite forms of divination. The practice allows you to truly delve deep within your psyche and connect with your intuition.

When you read during a cleromancy session you tend to pick up things you normally wouldn't pick up in a tarot reading. Why? Because the bones, baubles, and curios that are cast out before you reveal something deeper: they reveal a story, a map that can pick up details that might be too deeply hidden in the standard tarot pack.

When you throw lots, you're delving into a psychic space that peers through the veil, beyond this mundane world into something deep and arcane. When preparing for a cleromancy or bone reading you should first get into the proper headspace (this should actually be applied to all readings). Take a few moments for yourself and try to quiet your mind. It may be helpful to play some soft meditation music, light your favorite incense, or burn herbs associated with divination and psychic/spirit work such as mugwort. Once you've gotten in the headspace it's time to prepare your setup and reading space.

Set up a table and lay out your casting cloth. A casting cloth can be of a single, solid color or it can have a design—perhaps even images you have drawn on yourself. You can also use one of the boards included at the back of this book.

You may wish to close your eyes and do a small invocation or prayer prior to performing the reading, asking for protection and calling in any ancestors, spirit guides, or deities you or the person you're reading for is connected to or works with.

To begin a reading, place your bones, baubles, or crystals in a bowl, large shell, or pouch—whichever you wish to use when tossing or casting the lots. While the object you toss the bones from is a personal choice, I have found it easier to cast from a bowl or medium-large abalone shell.

There are several ways to cast lots prior to the reading, and at the end of the day, the method you choose is up to you, as the reader. Whether you have the querent bundle and throw the lots in a reading is a personal choice and will not affect the accuracy of the reading.

When the session is over be sure to thank the tools you were working with and then the ancestors, spirit guides, and deities you invoked for being part of your session.

## METHOD 1

Ask the querent to think about a question as you shake the bones, using your hands to stop bones from escaping. When the querent has thought of their question, have them say "Throw" as you toss the bones upon the mat.

## METHOD 2

Allow the querent to meditate on their question while they hold and shake the lots. Instruct them to toss the lots upon the mat when they've finished thinking about their question.

## METHOD 3

Have the querent close their eyes and meditate on their question and then reach in and pick a handful of items from the bowl, shell, or pouch and scatter the items on the mat.

# CLEANSING AND CONSECRATION RITE

Cleansing your space and tools is extremely important, especially when the space or tools will be used for magic or divination of any kind. Consecration is to many holy or magical, because it gives the tools a charged purpose.

This basic rite is intended to cleanse and purify your casting set; this removes any negative and unwanted energies that may be lingering on the objects and makes them ready for divinatory use. You can perform this rite for any and all magical tools you wish to cleanse and consecrate. Perform this rite at midnight on a full or dark moon for an added magical measure.

YOU WILL NEED:

| |
|---|
| Your tools |
| Lighter or matches |
| 1 white candle |
| Patchouli incense and burner |
| 1 bell |
| 3 pinches of salt |
| Small bowl of water |

## STEP 5

Once all objects have been passed through, hold them in your hands, blow into them and say: *These bones are of earth and spirit, those deserving of fortunes are sure to hear it.*

## STEP 6

Snuff out the candle, burn or discard the spell remnants, and sleep with your casting stones under your pillow or mattress for three nights to deepen your relationship with them. Pay attention to your dreams during this time.

## STEP 1

Gather the tools you wish to cleanse and place them before you. Light the candle and say: *Darkness now comes to light and thus begins this sacred rite.*

## STEP 2

Burn the incense and ring the bell three times, saying: *By power of air, and the knell of the bell all malefic spirits and energies I dispel.*

## STEP 3

Add three pinches of salt to the bowl of water and say: *Earth to water, thrice about. All malefic spirits I drive out.*

## STEP 4

Pass the objects chosen for your casting kit one at a time through the flame of the candle, then the smoke of the incense, and then finally sprinkle with the salt water and say: *By fire, air, water, and earth, I give you new purpose and new birth.*

# PROTECTION RITUAL

This protection ritual is derived from a 17th-century ritual that was, ironically enough, used to protect oneself against magic and witchcraft. This ritual is intended to be performed before or after casting fortunes.

Know that you do not have to perform this ritual after every reading, but that when performing readings, you make yourself vulnerable to outside forces as well as other people's energies. This is a good ritual to do once a month or so, to build spiritual and magical wards that will shield you from negative energies and intrusive spirits or people. Remember, you must always be protected spiritually when performing a reading.

### YOU WILL NEED:

| |
| --- |
| Equal parts rue, agrimony, yarrow |
| 4 white chime candles |
| 3 drops olive oil |
| Lighter or matches |

**STEP 1**
Mix the herbs together and sprinkle the mixture into an equal-armed cross.

**STEP 2**
Place candles at each of the four points of the cross.

**STEP 3**
Use the remaining mixture to sprinkle a circle around the cross and candles.

**STEP 4**
Anoint each candle with some olive oil.

**STEP 5**
Light the candles and say: *I strip malevolence of its power, here and now, and every hour. I banish spirits of negativity and ask all fearsome folk to promptly flee. Primordial spirits of earth and my ancestors, please protect me. As I will, so it shall be.*

**STEP 6**
Allow the candles to burn down completely and then sweep up and bury the remaining spell contents in your backyard or on and around your property.

Rue

Agrimony

Yarrow

## CHAPTER TWO

# NECROMANCY

The very word "necromancy" can send shivers down one's spine. Today most people think of zombies or being able to control a legion of the undead when they think of the word. This is partly because of its use in pop culture, like in the famous role-playing game Dungeons and Dragons. However, necromancy is not about reviving or reanimating the dead, but rather communicating with and through the dead.

The word "necromancy" derives from the Ancient Greek word *necro* meaning "death." This form of divination and magic has been around for centuries and was prevalent during antiquity. Necromancy is even spoken of in the Bible (1 Sam 25:1; 28:3), in which King Saul seeks out a witch known for her gifts of necromancy to summon forth the spirit of the prophet Samuel in hopes of gaining answers about an upcoming battle. In Homer's *Odyssey*, the demi-goddess and witch, Circe, was skilled in necromancy and even taught Odysseus her gifts so that he could journey to the underworld and seek out the spirit of a prophet for assistance in getting back home.

Death is a natural and unavoidable part of life, but science has proven that energy cannot be destroyed, only altered and changed. This concept is what necromancy is based off of; that the energy of one's spirit can still be harnessed and utilized for answers and magical workings long after the physical body has left this realm. Necromancy is an umbrella term that covers spirit communication (also known as mediumship), channeling spirits through tools such as a pendulum, or utilizing bones for divinatory purposes such as cleromancy. Spirit work in spells and witchery also constitutes necromancy.

While the practice of necromancy is not required in order to cast fortunes or perform cleromancy, it is relevant if you incorporate any bones in your casting kit,

or even shells and roots, for they also have spirits and energies. This is animism, the concept that every living thing has a soul or spirit. Under the belief of animism any shell, plant, or natural thing would have a surviving essence, even after it has passed. This essence can be tapped into by siphoning the energy from its remains. Hence a bone could be utilized in necromancy to contact a specific spirit. Bones in readings act almost like magnets, attracting the related spirit energies.

When you read with bones, you're not only using the bone as a tool, but almost as a companion in the reading. You're utilizing the energy of the animal whose spirit resides within the bones. This essentially makes bone reading a way to also communicate with spirit allies. Necromancy does not require the use of bones in order to be performed, however; necromancy is simply connecting to the spirit realm. You can use tarot, pendulums, scrying, and many other tools alongside the art of necromancy.

When you start working with spirits, it is important to state your intention to work with them and to set clear boundaries. Remember that necromancy is a partnership with spirits and the netherworld. We are asking the spirits of the dead to assist us; they are not under servitude and we must approach them with respect. Always thank the spirits and bones for their efforts and messages after you have finished your divination session.

Incorporating necromancy into your divinatory and reading work is not for the faint of heart, nor for skeptics.

If you do not believe in spirits, or that the soul of the dearly departed can linger on after death, then it will be quite hard to work this practice into your readings. With that being said, it is important to develop a connection to and relationship with the dead and spirits before even trying to work them into your readings.

An easy way to begin building a relationship with spirits and the dead is by working with your bones. Spend time with each and every bone that you decide to use in your cleromancy arsenal. Ask yourself why you picked that specific bone. Meditate and spend time with a certain bone. What does it mean to you? What does the energy and symbolism of that animal signify to you? How did you come across the bone?

Look through your bones and connect with the spirit of the animal by thinking of its living state, and what the bone and its energy is supplying to your readings. Perhaps do a gratitude ritual for the animal and its spirit. You can easily do this for all your bones by simply holding the bones in your hands, bringing them close to your chest, and thanking the animal and its spirit for finding its way to you, as well as for its assistance in your readings.

You will also want to build a relationship with all spirits, including your ancestors. This can be done by creating a simple ancestral altar consisting of a few pictures, mementos, or belongings of ancestors, followed by candles, a favorite item, and perhaps an alcoholic beverage or candy as an offering.

# NECROMANCY INCENSE

This simple mixture can be burned on a charcoal disk or used to dress a candle during divination to further enhance your connection to the spirit realm and invite spirits to the reading. For added benefits, make the mixture during a dark moon, sacred to Hecate, the primordial Greco-Roman goddess of magic, the crossroads, and necromancy.

**YOU WILL NEED:**

1 tbsp mugwort

1 tbsp wormwood

1 tsp mullein

1 tsp earth from a cemetery (rosemary can be substituted)

**STEP 1**

Assemble your ingredients. One by one, take an ingredient and give it thanks silently or out loud. This is acknowledging the spirit and essence of the natural ingredient that will be assisting in making your incense. Add it to the bowl.

**STEP 2**

Mix the ingredients together. When you've finished mixing, close your eyes, place both hands over the bowl of ingredients and lightly breathe over the incense, thus giving it life and your personal essence. Burn the incense on a charcoal disk. You can easily find self-lighting charcoal disks made specifically for incense at most occult-metaphysical stores and online.

# NECROMANCY RITUAL TO CONNECT WITH YOUR BONES

This simple ritual can be performed to enhance your spiritual connection to your bones and curio. It can be done once with all your bones, or every time you add a new bone to your reading set.

### YOU WILL NEED:

A bowl of spring water

1 tsp honey

1 tsp milk

1 pinch mugwort

A lighter or matches

1 black chime candle

Bones

Paper towel or rag

### STEP 1

In a bowl of water add the honey, milk, and mugwort and mix together with your fingers.

### STEP 2

Light the chime candle, stare at the flame and say: *By the primordial forces, known and unknown, I enchant each stone, root, and bone.*

### STEP 3

Take a bone, sprinkle it with the mixture from the bowl and say: *I take this relic filled with death ...* Now, inhale deeply and then breathe heavily on the bone and say: *And enchant with life with my very breath*

### STEP 4

Pass the bone quickly through the flame and say: *By sacred fire I consecrate thee to cast my fortunes truthfully with the wisdom of spirit, so mote it be.*

### STEP 5

Wipe the bones down with a paper towel or rag and allow the candle to burn down completely. Leave the bowl out for the remainder of the evening and on the following day, pour the remaining mixture in your front or backyard or down the sink, thanking the spirits.

# CHAPTER THREE

# SCRYING

Do you ever see shapes and figures in clouds? How about a popcorn ceiling?

Or did you ever search for words in alphabet soup as a child?

If so, you've taken the first step in an ancient form of

divination known as scrying.

Scrying is a method of prophetic foresight that relies upon the symbols and images that appear from looking at certain things, such as tea, coffee, fire, glass, clouds, and, well, even possibly cereal, soup, or a ceiling. The form of scrying many of us are most familiar with is probably crystal gazing, in part due to the crystal ball-reading psychic whose image lives in all of our minds.

The word "scrying" derives from the Old English *descry*, meaning "to make out dimly" or "to reveal." The word itself shows that, as with casting lots, scrying involves the reader interpreting images and peering through the shadows to find the meaning or answers hidden in what they are looking at. As readers, we rely on our intuition and second sight being triggered and enhanced when we peer into the imagery and begin to scry. Scrying is a helpful and potent way of activating our second sight, that part within us that allows us to sense things beyond what we are normally used to sensing. Scrying is more than just a way to "foretell the future"; it is a method of gazing at a particular thing or group of things and being able to reveal the message hidden within them.

Due to the nature of casting lots and the process of reading them, this form of divination falls under the category of scrying. Also, like casting lots and cleromancy, scrying is centuries old and a version of it had been practiced by every culture around the world. The Ancient

Egyptians used oil or ink in water to scry, while the Greeks and Romans would read the innards of sacrificial animals, as well as throw knucklebones. French astrologer Nostradamus (1503–66) and English alchemist John Dee (1527–1608) were each said to scry with a slap of black obsidian. In Salem, Massachusetts in 1692, a group of girls got together and attempted to find out about each other's love lives by utilizing "The Venus Glass" (also known as oomancy) by pouring egg whites in a glass of warm water and reading the shapes the whites created. This harmless form of divination would be recorded by Reverend Hale and become a key instrument in what would later be known as the Salem witch trials. Today, Indigenous Americans read signs in smoke, and Santería Ifá religious readings are conducted with coconut shells and bones.

Scrying is a wonderful form of divination for those who are imaginative and may struggle with fixed divination systems such as tarot or runes, which often require memorization and practice. Scrying only requires an understanding of symbology and the ability to see figures and shapes within objects, as well as an open mind. To begin scrying, start by looking at different things: the surfaces of wood, your ceiling, the bubbles appearing in your fresh hot cup of morning coffee, or the swirls and shapes that appear when you pour in some milk or cream. What figures and shapes do you see?

In most cases scrying is used on reflective surfaces such as water, oil, crystals, or glass, but there are actually no limitations for the medium in which scrying can be utilized (remember, popcorn ceiling). You could even close your eyes and try to interpret the shapes that appear against your inner eyelids—eyelid scrying, anyone?

While scrying can be performed simply by gazing at a chosen medium and finding the images within, there are also ritualistic methods that can be used to help enhance the scrying session by falling into a self-induced, trancelike state. This can be achieved by repeating a few words like a mantra, through meditation, or by staring blankly at your chosen medium and allowing your mind to disengage. Performing a spell or ritual can sometimes enhance the scrying process, or you may wish to burn incense or light candles to get into the mood, but this is all relative to the reader and what feels comfortable to you as an individual.

Here are two easy scrying techniques to try out for yourself or another. Remember to relax and trust your intuition. I find that it's best to keep a notebook close by and write down the images I see so that I may refer to them later and figure out additional meanings. *The Element Encyclopedia of Secret Signs and Symbols* by Adele Nozedar is a wonderful resource for looking up the symbolism and meaning behind any imagery you might see.

# VENUS GLASS

This 17th-century scrying method was used to inquire about matters of the heart (Venus being the planet and Roman goddess associated with love, and eggs being associated with fertility). While you could use this method of scrying for any scenario, for this example we will stick to a reading surrounding love.

YOU WILL NEED:

A clear glass

Warm water

1 egg

Notebook and pen

**STEP 1**
Fill the glass with warm water.

**STEP 2**
Hold the egg between both hands, close your eyes, and think of what you'd like to look at in regard to love. This could be a current or future relationship, a specific person of interest, areas of love to focus on, etc.

**STEP 3**
Crack the egg on the glass and carefully pour the white of the egg into the water, ensuring none of the yolk slips through.

**STEP 4**
Allow the whites to sit in the warm water for several minutes.

**STEP 5**
After they take shape, study the whites and write down the images you see within the glass.

**STEP 6**
Think of your question and the images that perhaps pertain to what you asked. Did you ask how you might meet a romantic partner? The appearance of a ship could indicate that this might happen on a trip, for example. Did you see a dog? Perhaps you'll meet someone who has a dog, or is quite loyal and trustworthy.

# OIL AND WATER SCRYING

This form of scrying dates back to the ancient Greeks and Egyptians
during the Hellenistic era (323–32 BCE). It has been used ever since and
has been quite reliable for me in my practice.

**YOU WILL NEED:**

A black or dark-colored bowl

Water

1 tbsp oil (olive, vegetable, sunflower, etc.)

Candles

**STEP 1**
Pour the water into the bowl and add the tablespoon of oil.

**STEP 2**
Light a few candles and dim or turn off the lights.

**STEP 3**
Place the candles close to the bowl of water and oil.

**STEP 4**
Allow your mind to clear. You may wish to play drumming
or meditation music to help you fall into a trancelike state.

**STEP 5**
Stare at the bowl and peer through the darkness, paying
attention to the images you see.

**STEP 6**
After the session, write down any symbols or images you
saw and attempt to interpret them.

# CUP READING

As we have discovered previously, scrying is the art of seeking prophetic insight within the images we see on surfaces. While many restrict scrying to reflective or flat surfaces, in reality scrying can be done with almost anything.

While tea leaf reading is often put in its own category known as tasseography or tasseomancy, the art of reading tea and coffee grounds requires scrying because you are looking at a surface and seeking prophetic insight from the shapes, formations, and images that appear in the clumping of tea or coffee.

Cups have been used for divination since the invention of drinking cups and bowls, as scrying is probably the oldest form of divination. While many attribute the invention of tea leaf reading to China because that's where tea was first commercially grown, there are accounts of similar "scrying in cups" methods from in and around Scotland, Ireland, and England way before trade with Asia developed, likely using herbal teas or decoctions. Cup readings are also found in the Middle East, where they used coffee as opposed to tea.

Like most forms of divination, cup readings vary in method, depending on the culture and region. Cup readings are less formal than other divinatory methods and don't require much ritual aside from the process of setting up and performing the reading. Cup readings are great to perform during social gatherings and can be quite fun to dish out, however don't be surprised if serious things appear in the reading. The purpose of cup readings in general is to look at the future prospects of the person whose cup is being read. Cup readings can be done with tea or coffee but it must be loose, as the grains, grounds, and kernels are what is read. Cup readings are performed after a person has drunk their tea or coffee; the remnants of what's left behind is then interpreted. Some cups are designed using specific images, astrological signs, and symbols to help the diviner read the patterns left behind by the tea or coffee, but for the most part, cup readings are performed in any cup, though a rounded cup is preferred.

There are different methods of cup readings and I encourage you to explore one that works for you. The method provided here is one that I learned years ago and still use to this day. As always, trust your intuition and be ready to look up any symbols or images that stand out to you and which may require deeper insight. You can also reference the list of symbols in this book for cup readings as well as any other scrying methods.

# CUP READING RITUAL

This is a basic method for divination via coffee or tea. Note here that while the coffee or tea is consumed, the purpose is not for taste but part of the reading ritual.

YOU WILL NEED:

Cup

Tea or coffee

Saucer

Notepaper and pen

### STEP 1
Put a pinch of coffee or tea into the cup.

### STEP 2
Pour boiling water into the cup and allow to steep for three minutes or so.

### STEP 3
Drink the tea or coffee, allowing the leaves or grounds to stay in the cup, straining with your teeth if necessary. A tiny bit of liquid should also be left in the cup.

### STEP 4
With your left hand, hold the cup by the handle and swirl the cup and remaining contents around three times in a quick motion.

### STEP 5
Quickly and carefully flip the cup over on the saucer and rotate the cup three times clockwise.

### STEP 6
Lift the cup from the saucer and look at the debris from the tea or coffee left in the cup.

### STEP 7
For cup reading, I like to divide the cup into three sections. The rim of the cup represents the present, the sides of the cup represent the future and things to come, and the bottom of the cup represents distant future. Images and tea clumped closer to the handle indicate the sooner you are to achieving that which you desire.

### STEP 8
Pay attention to any symbols you see. Write them down and interpret them as best you can.

# SCRYING SYMBOLISM

Searching for symbols while scrying can be fun, but also strenuous. When we do see images, we often fall short on what the images mean and the prophetic energies behind said symbols. To help ease the burden, here is a list of popular images that pop up in scrying sessions and can be referenced when doing cup readings, egg readings, or any other form of scrying.

This list is by no means an authority on the matter and only reflects a fraction of the images and the symbolism out there. The interpretation of symbols is relative at best. If you have a personal connection to an image or symbol you see and feel called to give it a different meaning when it appears in a reading, feel free to.

**Acorn:** success and gain: good health

**Anchor:** stability, constancy, grounded

**Apple:** knowledge, achievement, health

**Axe:** difficulties, attack, need for action

**Baby:** something new, pregnancy, children

**Bell:** harmony, celebration, creation, faith, unexpected news

**Birds:** ascension, good news, travel, omen

**Boat:** life path, journey, visit from a friend or family

**Book:** answers found: if open, it's good news; if closed, you need to investigate something

**Butterfly:** transition, transformation, Butterfly Effect

**Candle:** faith, hope, spirituality, help from others

**Cat:** deceit, a false friend, magic, sorcery, jinx, magic worked on you

**Chain:** ancestors, engagement, a wedding, chain link, karma, promises made or broken (depending on if link intact or broken)

**Chair:** a guest, rest, support

**Circle:** success, completion, renewal

**Clock:** time, better health, sooner rather than later

**Coin:** change in financial status, wealth, prosperity

**Cross:** protection, sacrifice, faith

**Cup:** reward, bloodlines, intuition

**Dagger:** warning, danger from self or others, power, attack

**Dog:** friend, loyalty, Sirius (the star and celestial connotation), Egyptian god (Anubis)

**Door:** opening (to something new) or closing (old issues and relations), spiritual (portal)

**Duck:** money coming, a man named Bill, "ducks in a row"

**Egg:** fertility, good omens, creation, new beginnings, birth, new opportunity

**Elephant:** wisdom, strength, luck, Hindu god (Ganesh), memory

**Envelope:** message coming, positive or negative

**Eye:** intuition and psychic insight: open (awakening); closed (something not seen)

**Fan:** discretion, comfort, concealing feelings

**Feather:** ascension, air, gentleness

**Fence:** limitations, minor setbacks, restrictions

**Fish:** Pisces, good fortune, movement

**Forked line:** speak with false tongue, false flattery, decision, at an impasse

**Fruit:** fruitful, prosperity, seeds being planted

**Gate:** opportunity, future success, portal, doorway, journey

**Goat:** fertility, witchcraft, magic, sexuality

**Gun:** anger, violence, fight, theft

**Hammer:** hard work needed, getting a point across, authority

**Hand:** creation: if open, means friendship; if closed, means an argument

**Hat:** head, consciousness, improvement, protection

**Hawk:** Egyptian god (Horus), insight, swiftness, action

**Heart:** romance, pleasure, love, trust, compassion, health

**Horse:** travel, good news, freedom

**Horseshoe:** good luck, attraction

**Hourglass:** time running out, need to decide something, synchronicity, illusion, creation

**House:** security, homecoming

**Kite:** wishes coming true, flying free, fun, friendship

**Knife:** broken friendship, hidden enemy

**Ladder:** promotion, a rise or fall in life, DNA

**Leaf:** new life, growth, nurture

**Lines:** if straight, means progress; if wavy, means uncertain path

**Lion:** strength, authority

**Lock:** obstacles, secrets, opposition, boundaries

**Mask:** something hidden, deceit, falsehood, false friends

**Mountain:** obstacles or journey

**Mouse:** theft, messiness, chaos

**Nail:** injustice, unfairness, ending, pain

**Oak tree:** health, long life, tree of life

**Owl:** gossip, scandal, owl symbology

**Question mark:** need for caution, uncertainty, missing person

**Rabbit:** need for bravery, time, fertility

**Raven:** prophecy, warning, bad news, unanswered questions

**Ring:** promises, commitment, coming full circle, near the top means marriage or the offer of marriage; if broken, means engagement broken off or false promises

**Rose:** love, beauty, romance

**Scale:** legal issues; if balanced, means just result; if unbalanced, means unjust result

**Scissors:** quarrels, possible separation

**Shell:** good news, feminine energy, guarded emotions

**Snake:** renewal, wisdom, or if the snake is attacking, an enemy, cunning

**Spider:** weaving together, plans being made, creativity

**Star:** health and happiness, hope, heavens, Egyptian deities (Isis and other goddesses), female energies

**Sun:** happiness, success, power, male deities

**Sword:** victory, success

**Tortoise:** patience, slow moving (Earth)

**Tree:** improvements, of life, creation, growth, your life path

**Wheel:** if complete, means good fortune; if broken, means disappointment

**Wolf:** ego, confidence, pride, alpha

## CHAPTER FOUR
# PENDULUMS

A pendulum is a suspended object that can be crafted from various materials such as a ring tied by a thread, or a crystal suspended by a chain, which has become more popular today. There are a variety of pendulums available for divinatory use. While many are made from various crystals, other materials include brass and silver, wood, and sometimes even a charm. You can easily create your own pendulum by tying a key, charm, ring, or stone to a cord or thread.

The pendulum has been used for centuries by mystics and magical practitioners alike. The first record of pendulums being used for divination dates all the way back to 4000 BCE in Ancient Greece. Pendulums were also utilized by the ancient Egyptians and ancient Romans and became a prized divinatory tool during the 19th-century spiritualist movement. Modern mystics use pendulums to answer yes/no questions, feel the presence of spirits, or help pick out tarot cards. Pendulums are said to connect with your higher self and the unseen world, helping you to pick up the energies around you. They are also great tools to utilize alongside spirit boards and divination grids, oftentimes called pendulum boards.

The use of the pendulum is also known as dowsing. This involves an object such as a stick, rod, or pendulum being pointed or directed in a certain way by energies or unseen forces in response to a question, which then guides the querent towards a specific path or answer. Aside from spiritual purposes, pendulum dowsing has also been utilized to find water sources, missing objects, and buried treasure, to predict the weather, and to determine the sex of unborn children.

Consult a pendulum any time you feel like you are uncertain about a situation, or perhaps need to be guided by spirit. The pendulum is a wonderful tool to use when you wish to communicate with deities, spirit guides, angelic beings, or even your higher self. If you're unsure of who or what to contact or connect with, simply try to let your mind go blank and ask nature, the universe, or a spirit to direct you.

The easiest way to connect and work with a pendulum is by simply allowing it to swing freely and guide you. If you decide to use the pendulum without a grid, you should first decide how you wish it to communicate with you. While suspending the pendulum between your fingers, allow it to hang freely and then ask it to show you yes/no/maybe/not at this time. Take note of each direction the pendulum swings, so that you know what the answers will be when you ask specific questions.

Think of the pendulum as an extension of yourself, a piece of you that is connected to the unknown that can draw wisdom from the supernatural energies you're trying to connect to and get answers from.

# PENDULUM DOWSING

To utilize a pendulum for divination, the first thing you'll need to do is build a connection with the tool. Hold the pendulum in your dominant hand and breathe lightly on it. You may also wish to give it a name to further enhance your spiritual bond and give it life.

The simplest method to begin using a pendulum is to suspend the pendulum from your thumb and index finger and ask the pendulum to show you what different answers look like. First ask the pendulum to show you a "Yes" answer. Allow the pendulum to swing freely and pay attention to the direction it goes: this will be how the pendulum says yes. Continue to repeat this method for "No" and "Maybe." Remember these movements and register them as the answers the pendulum gives.

While the pendulum is not restricted to yes/no readings, those are probably the best questions to start out with, as it is a way to grow a stronger bond between you and the pendulum. A greater way to expand your pendulum use is to utilize pendulum boards, grids, or charts that are designed to give more detailed answers to other questions you may have outside of the basic yes/no.

To read a board using a pendulum, hover the pendulum over the board and ask your question. Take a deep breath and allow the pendulum to guide your hand across the board. Pay attention to the weight of the pendulum: it may drop down or you might feel a pull or tug. Allow the pendulum to swing naturally, noticing where on the board the pendulum swings. Then look at the words or symbols on the board and see how that relates to your question.

Remember that, like most spiritual and magical tools, you will probably wish to cleanse your pendulum before and in between uses. This can be done simply by sprinkling the pendulum with a few drops of salt water, or with a smoke cleansing through the use of incense or herb bundles such as cedar, rue, or rosemary (see pages 36–37).

When your pendulum is not in use, keep it in a small pouch or box on your altar or carry it on your person. The more you engage with and practice using your pendulum, the stronger your connection will get and the more accurate your readings will be.

## THE OBJECTS

While any object or material may be used to create a fine working pendulum, different materials and components will hold different energies. Here's a look at the most common pendulums and their properties.

**Brass**
To connect to unseen natural forces and pick up on energies.

**Wood**
To connect to nature, natural energies, and spirits. Helps to ground and center.

**Amethyst**
For psychic enhancement. Helps fine-tune your intuition and open your spiritual senses.

**Clear Quartz**
Amplifies energies and magic, great for getting to the root of problems and issues.

**Black Obsidian**
For protection or banishing, preferable for readings that might be emotionally strenuous.

## CHAPTER FIVE
# OTHER FORMS OF DIVINATION

While this book focuses primarily on cleromancy and bone casting, there are other forms of divination that are just as powerful and potent and will work in tandem with the divinatory methods taught in this book. You will find that the other forms of divination mentioned herein complement the primary subject of this book. Scrying, for instance, requires the reader to look beyond the mundane, finding symbols and interpreting omens within different surfaces or amongst random objects. Therefore, scrying is a wonderful skill to layer with cleromancy and bone casting, as you can scry amongst the random lots and bones that are scattered on a board.

These other methods are being explored here so that you as the reader can look at similar forms of divination and add the ones that work for you to your repertoire. The other reason to showcase alternative divination systems is because many of the boards featured within this book are multifunctional and suitable for various divination systems and tools, such as cartomancy (reading with cards) or dowsing with a pendulum. Other obscure forms of divination are brought to light within these pages, such as oomancy (egg divination), which not only is considered a form of scrying, but also a form of spiritual cleansing. Knowing these other forms of divination allows you to truly understand the spiritual realm, as well as unlock your intuition. You will also find that knowing one of these divinatory methods will allow you to connect to other methods mentioned in this book. Think of these different divinatory systems as complementary to each other.

When learning divination, the thing to keep in mind is that you must not only trust your intuition, but you must also learn to read the signs and symbols revealed to you and remember their meanings. While intuition is a major part of divination, so is learning to understand the tools and interpret their meanings. You will find that

several of the methods mentioned in this book are "fixed" systems, meaning that the tools are meant to be studied and read appropriately with very little room for variation. Fixed divinatory systems such as runes are meant to be read in accordance with the question answered or the spread in which the runes are cast. With fixed systems like these, intuition only serves as a way to expand on the reading, but never to change the meaning or influence of the tools and their fixed meanings. For example, the Three of Swords in tarot represents heartbreak and disappointment. While the meaning can be altered based on the position of the card or in accordance to the question at hand, the Three of Swords cannot be interpreted as something vastly different than what the card is supposed to mean.

The divination systems in this book are a mix of fixed and intuitive. Even cleromancy, which is for the most part intuitive, can be made a fixed system when you designate specific meanings to the bones and curio in your cleromancy set. This chapter reveals several types of divination systems that will work alongside cleromancy and bone casting. Read through them, explore the different methods, and see if any call to you.

# ASTRAGALOMANCY

Ah, yes, the ancient art of astragalomancy. Try saying that out loud.
Sounds fun, right? Well, while the name seems pretty obscure and
complicated, this divination practice is actually quite common and a bit
more simple than most, once you get used to it.

Astragalomancy is the use of bones and/or dice for divinatory purposes. Back in antiquity the dice were originally just knucklebones or vertebra from animals, usually livestock such as sheep or cattle. In fact, the Greek word *astragalos* means both dice and knucklebone. Marked knucklebones and dice found in Athens near a temple of Aphrodite date back to 500 BCE. Oftentimes numbers and symbols were marked on the bones that corresponded to a letter or word that was interpreted by the diviner in accordance with the question that was asked. Another method of reading the bones and dice is the one used in this book for cleromancy. The dice are thrown, and the reader dictates the answer according to where the dice fall on the layout. Pay attention to any patterns that form, such as which side revealed itself face up, how far apart the bones are to each other, and how close they are to the person asking the question.

By the early 14th century, dice, gambling, and games of chance had taken Europe by storm. Dice became ever-popular as a means of gambling, as well as fortune telling. To this day dice are used by some readers and are often found in a bone throwing/cleromancy kit.

# MODERN DICE DIVINATION METHOD

YOU WILL NEED:

Pen

Paper

A pair of dice

## STEP 1
Write 20 random answers and/or prophecies that come to your mind. (Examples: success is yours, better luck next time, good fortune will arrive soon, bad luck is around you, etc.)

## STEP 2
Number the phrases 4–24.

## STEP 3
Shake and roll a pair of dice, add the numbers together, and then write them down.

## STEP 4
Cast the dice a second time, then add those numbers together.

## STEP 5
Add the numbers of both rolls together and use the resulting number to find the corresponding answer on the numbered list you made.

## Simple Yes/No dice reading
Meditate on a yes/no question and roll a pair of dice. Even numbers mean yes, and an odd number indicates no.

# OOMANCY

From Ancient Rome to modern America, eggs have been used for a variety of magical and divinatory purposes in many different cultures. Eggs take center stage in many pagan myths, religious ceremonies, and holidays, including Samhain, an ancient Celtic holiday and precursor to Halloween in which the druids (Celtic priests) would divine with eggs to foretell the length of winter, as well as receive messages from their beloved dead in the other world.

In ancient Germanic paganism the egg was a symbol of Eostre, the goddess of spring. Eggs would be decorated and colored with paprika and spices and left as offerings to ensure a bountiful year. The cosmic egg is also a central theme in many creation myths detailing how the world was born. The popularity of eggs in paganism and folk magic makes sense because it is the physical representation of the cycle of life. Naturally it would be a great divination tool because of its symbolism: birth, growth, development, and nature.

Eggs have also been used to cleanse and heal in folk magic throughout the world. In fact, the word "oomancy" does not mean only using eggs for divination, but for spiritual cleansing as well. *Oon* is the Ancient Greek word for egg. While the practice of egg divination has become widespread, it is thought to have originated in Ancient Greece and was adopted and popularized by the Romans.

In Santería, eggs are used to remove the negative spiritual vibrations of a person and leave them cleansed and purified by rolling the egg carefully over the person's entire body, and then cracking it and reading the yolk to see what ails them or what additional spellwork may be needed to improve the person's current situation. Methods like this are found in various other practices such as hoodoo, brujería, rootwork, and conjure. Like cleromancy and bone throwing, there is no one right way to perform egg divination. Each variation is tied to either a specific culture, stems from a historical text or folk practice, or is passed down through generations of family members. One of the most popular forms of oomancy is perhaps best known because of its appearance in the Salem witch trials of 1692. Known as the Venus Glass and mentioned in this book, this version of oomancy reveals not only potential love interests but can also be quite predictive in other ways.

# EGG CLEANSING AND READING

In this simple cleansing ritual, an egg is used to draw out your negative energies and utilize them in a reading.

### YOU WILL NEED:

Incense (to cleanse) such as frankincense, myrrh, rosemary, or dragon's blood

Incense holder

Matches or lighter

Clear bowl or glass of warm water

1 egg, preferably chicken

### STEP 1
Light your incense and pass the egg through the smoke a few times to cleanse the egg.

### STEP 2
Starting at the crown of your head, roll the egg gently down one side of your body. As you do so, visualize the egg absorbing all your negative thoughts, stress, anxiety, ailments, or anything else that is negative in your life.

### STEP 3
Continue rolling the egg around you until you feel satisfied that it has absorbed enough of the negative vibrations that perhaps are within you. When you have finished, crack open the egg and allow the contents to spill into the bowl or glass of warm water.

### STEP 4
Pay attention to the shapes, bubbles, and formations that appear in the glass or bowl.

### STEP 5
When you have finished reading the egg, dispose of it by tossing the egg and water out and away from your property, preferably at a crossroads, train tracks, at a tree, or at the gates of a cemetery.

### THINGS TO LOOK FOR

✳ The appearance of an eye is an indication that the evil eye has been cast upon you and suggests an additional cleansing is needed.

✳ A foul odor, blood, discoloring of yolk, or a black spot is an indication of a curse, hex, or other malefic magic put upon you.

✳ Bubbles indicate ancestors and spirit guides surrounding and protecting you.

✳ A double yolk is the all-around sign of good luck and good fortune. If you are pregnant or trying to be, it could indicate potential for good things, or a potential marriage if you're currently dating someone.

✳ No yolk inside the egg is universally seen as a bad omen. Deeper cleansing, uncrossing, and/or protective magic should be performed immediately.

✳ Seeing a face indicates that someone you love may be upset with you.

✳ Seeing animals should be interpreted with the spiritual and symbolic aspects of that animal.

# ASTROLOGY

Astrology, or "the study of the stars," is a system that studies the placements and movements of celestial bodies and how they influence the human experience on Earth. Part science, part psychology, it can help us find meaning in our life, gain insight into our own potential, and show us the path that lies ahead. This tradition goes back thousands of years and transcends many cultures, and it has never been more popular than it is today.

Every astrology reading begins with a snapshot of the sky at a specific time and place called a "star chart." This is a circular map divided into 12 sections, which records the location of the main celestial bodies used in astrology. Those 12 sections are called "houses," and each house is associated with a specific sign of the zodiac.

Most of us are already familiar with the zodiac, as you've probably seen them online in your daily horoscope, or in magazines at the checkout counter. Each sign is a symbol, usually some sort of animal, representing a combination of traits, ideas, behaviors, and mythology. They are broken down by elements (Fire, Earth, Air, Water) and qualities or modes (Cardinal, Fixed, Mutable). These are quick ways of understanding the fundamental energy of each sign.

The main celestial bodies used in astrology are the seven planets (Mercury, Venus, Mars, Jupiter, Saturn, Uranus, and Neptune) and the dwarf planet Pluto; and the two luminaries—the Sun and the Moon. They are usually just all lumped together as "planets." Some people choose to include smaller celestial bodies such as Chiron, Vespa, or Lilith, but the planets are the most important. Symbolically, the planets, houses, and signs together illustrate one big picture that can tell many different stories. It all depends on the information you're looking for.

With such an expansive history, astrology can get complicated very quickly. So to keep things simple, these are the most important ideas to know:

* Each planet represents a different facet of our personality. These are things within ourselves, such as our identity, our values, our communication styles, our behavior, etc.
* Each house represents a different area of our life. This includes how you are in public, home life, your relationships, your career, etc.
* Each sign represents the energy expressed. How a planet acts and how a house is defined changes depending on the sign they fall under.
* Each planet, house, and zodiac sign have natural associations with each other, based on similar qualities or concepts. You'll see a lot of overlap with their information. They are not interchangeable, but if you can understand the signs, it will be easier to understand their respective planets and the houses as well.

Start your astrology journey by casting your own "natal chart," a star chart created by using your birth date, birth time, and birth location. You can easily do this for free online at *www.astro.com* or *www.astro-charts.com*. Make sure your birth details are accurate!

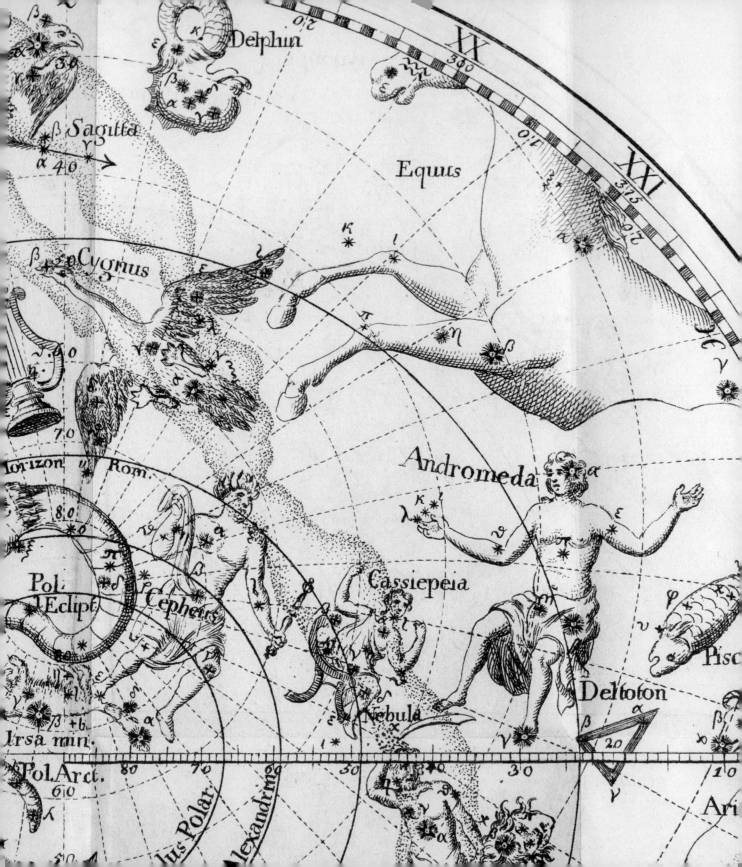

# PLANETS

| Planet | | Zodiac Sign(s) | Personality Facet |
|---|---|---|---|
| ☉ | Sun | Leo | Identity, ego, inner core, where you shine, guiding light, pride, highest potential |
| ☽ | Moon | Cancer | Emotions, intuition, expression of feelings, inner nature, home life, reactions |
| ☿ | Mercury | Gemini, Virgo | Communication, intellect, learning style, living preference, daily life, work habits |
| ♀ | Venus | Taurus, Libra | Love language, relationships, beauty, aesthetics, financial habits, personal style |
| ♂ | Mars | Aries | Drive, energy, sex drive, action, fighting spirit, courage, survival, strength, anger |
| ♃ | Jupiter | Sagittarius | Potential, luck, talent, growth opportunities, higher knowledge, value systems, hubris, ethics, abundance |
| ♄ | Saturn | Capricorn | Life lessons, hardships, struggles, restrictions, long-term achievements, boundaries, inner authority |
| ♅ | Uranus | Aquarius | Sense of freedom, eccentricity, technology, sudden changes, upheavals, politics, hopes, wishes |
| ♆ | Neptune | Pisces | Imagination, illusions/delusions, spirituality, beliefs, dreams, escapist tendencies, psychic matters, art |
| ♇ | Pluto | Scorpio | Transformations, rebirth, regeneration, deep changes, shared resources, sexual relationships, death |

# HOUSES

| House | Zodiac Sign | Planet | Area of Life |
|-------|-------------|--------|--------------|
| 1 | Aries | Mars | Identity, appearance, how the world sees you, mannerisms, first impressions |
| 2 | Taurus | Venus | Personal values, money, wealth, personal finances, material possessions, security needs, aesthetics, beauty, land ownership |
| 3 | Gemini | Mercury | Communication style, learning, education, neighborhood, siblings, short travel, locality, thinking and speaking style, language |
| 4 | Cancer | Moon | Home, family, personal history, maternal connections, childhood, heritage, ancestry, private world |
| 5 | Leo | Sun | Self-expression, love life, romance, creativity, sense of style, children, pleasure, artistry, games, amusement, holidays, risk-taking |
| 6 | Virgo | Mercury | Daily life, work habits, jobs, health, nutrition, routines, rituals, coworkers, well-being, fitness, pets, service |
| 7 | Libra | Venus | Relationships, partnerships, open enemies, marriage, contracts, legal issues, conflicts, justice, litigation |
| 8 | Scorpio | Pluto | Sex, joint resources, death, taxes, loans, wills, intimacy, taboos, legacies, occult, transformations |
| 9 | Sagittarius | Jupiter | Higher education, philosophy, religion, long-distance travel, spirituality, in-laws, foreign affairs, gambling, luck |
| 10 | Capricorn | Saturn | Career, ambition, public life, paternal connections, reputation, recognition, achievements, authority figures, status, government |
| 11 | Aquarius | Uranus | Friendships, social life, groups, clubs, societies, goals, wishes, originality |
| 12 | Pisces | Neptune | Karma, subconscious mind, deep healing, addictions, prisons, hospitals, secret enemies, sacrifices, undoing, self-destruction |

# ZODIAC SIGNS

| Zodiac Sign | Symbol | Planet(s) | Element | Quality/Mode | Traits/Ideas |
|---|---|---|---|---|---|
| Aries ♈ | Ram | Mars | Fire | Cardinal | Strength, vitality, warriors, anger, impulsive, extroverted, pioneering, competitive, childlike, survival, independent, spontaneous, self-motivated, initiative, risky, imposing, impatience, foolish, selfish, leadership, reckless |
| Taurus ♉ | Bull | Venus | Earth | Fixed | Calm, slow, physical work, materialistic, grounded, sensual, practical, down-to-earth, patient, possessive, security, money, endurance, persistence, gentle, lazy, greedy, resistant, stable, reliable, beauty, nature, primitive |
| Gemini ♊ | Twins | Mercury | Air | Mutable | Duality, intelligence, communicative, social, black-or-white thinking, adaptable, quick, logical, charming, curious, learning, diversity, restless, clever, wit, movement, changing, superficial, nervous, versatility, exchanges |
| Cancer ♋ | Crab | Moon | Water | Cardinal | Sensitive, emotional, tenacious, withdrawal, home, family, motherhood, self-protective, caregiving, receptive, empathetic, overbearing, sentimental, moody, intuition, comfort, nurturing, history, needy |
| Lco ♌ | Lion | Sun | Fire | Fixed | Charisma, royalty, bold, style, glamorous, theater, drama, generous, self-centered, creativity, pride, confidence, entertainment, rulership, loyalty, vanity, flattery, arrogance, affectionate, popularity, leisure |
| Virgo ♍ | Virgin | Mercury | Earth | Mutable | Function, efficiency, criticism, service-oriented, supportive, helpful, nursing, health, well-being, perfectionism, focus, humble, order, skill-building, crafty, worry, boring, analytical, improvements, detail-oriented, counseling |

| Zodiac Sign | Symbol | Planet(s) | Element | Quality/Mode | Traits/Ideas |
|---|---|---|---|---|---|
| Libra ♎ | Scales | Venus | Air | Cardinal | Balance, equality, relationships, diplomatic, justice, law, kindness, decisions, compromise, elegance, design, harmony, negotiation, fairness, dependent, conflict-averse, passive/aggressive, friendly, flirty, agreements |
| Scorpio ♏ | Scorpion | Pluto, Mars* | Water | Fixed | Intensity, depth, transformation, mystery, willpower, determination, secretive, private, honesty, regeneration, resilience, destruction, decay, death, sex, obsession, magnetic, vindictive, penetration, resentment, precision, debt |
| Sagittarius ♐ | Archer, Centaur | Jupiter | Fire | Mutable | Optimism, philosophy, religion, higher knowledge, travel, expansive, horizons, adventure, possibilities, exploration, blunt, judgmental, jovial, humor, wanderlust, truth, non-committal, morality, restlessness |
| Capricorn ♑ | Goat | Saturn | Earth | Cardinal | Hard work, business, achievement, ambition, success, professional, serious, depression, conservative, self-reliant, dignity, responsibility, fatherhood, concentration, obstacles, prosperity, coldness, caution, discipline, frugal |
| Aquarius ♒ | Water-bearer | Uranus, Saturn* | Air | Fixed | Progressive, humanitarian, environmental, unique, eccentricity, community, idealistic, unconventional, detachment, rebels, rule-breaking, enlightenment, unity, cooperation, paradox, futuristic, objective, invention, surprising, genius |
| Pisces ♓ | Fish | Neptune, Jupiter* | Water | Mutable | Divine, compassion, spirituality, sacrifice, subconscious, imagination, dreams, escapism, charity, retreat, fantasy, soulful, addictive tendencies, elusive, endings, psychic ability, transcendence, artistry, spirit world |

*Before Uranus, Neptune, and Pluto were discovered, some signs had different planetary "rulers." Some astrologers like to consider these alternative associations to further expand their readings.

# ASTROMANCY (ASTROLOGY-INSPIRED CLEROMANCY)

Astromancy is divination using the stars. Technically, you would use a star chart—like your natal chart—to make astrological predictions. Some methods include reading transits or calculating progressions, but these go beyond the scope of this book. Luckily, you do not have to dive too deep to use astrology in your divination practices.

This method blends classic cleromancy with the elements of astrology. This is best used for multi-faceted questions, or to see the bigger picture of a situation.

**STEP 1**

Use a 12-inch diameter standard blank astrology chart (such as the one on the next page) as your reading board. It might help to make sure the house numbers and traditional rulers (planets and signs) are included.

**STEP 2**

Create a set of ten items you can cast, each representing one of the planets. It can be anything, as long as it is small, durable, and easily identified: coins, shells, beads, trinkets, pebbles, bones, crystals, dice, rings, feathers, seeds, etc. Think outside the box! Place your items in a bowl or pouch, or just hold them all in your hands.

**Sample Set:**

*Sun: a piece of hard candy*
*Moon: a seashell*
*Mercury: a small sturdy feather*
*Venus: a large coin*
*Mars: a matchstick*
*Jupiter: a 6-sided die*
*Saturn: a simple ring*
*Uranus: a small battery*
*Neptune: an amethyst crystal*
*Pluto: a bone*

**STEP 3**

Ask your question. Keep it open-ended (not "yes or no") and be as specific as possible. Say it aloud or think it clearly as you gently shake the items in your hands or container.

**STEP 4**

Toss the items on the board. Take note of where the "planets" have fallen and use the tables provided to guide your interpretation.

**Troubleshooting**

✳ If some items touch or overlap, consider them within the same house/sign.

✳ If an item isn't on the board, go ahead and apply it to the closest house/sign or toss it again.

✳ For simpler questions, try using only the tokens that might be most relevant to your question. (Example: if your question is "What career should I pursue to get a higher paycheck?" only use the tokens for "Sun," "Venus," and "Saturn," which relate to "life purpose," "money matters," and "ambition," respectively.)

# RUNE CRAFT

Runes have been used by the Norse pagans for centuries. The earliest recorded use of them being used for divination is from 98 CE. The most common system of runes used today is known as the Elder Futhark. The Futhark is also an ancient system of writing, which holds much deeper meaning and symbolism. These meanings energetically change within the vast mysteries that manifest the patterns of the universe, as well as our personal understanding of them. When learned, properly read, and understood the runes reveal these patterns, teaching us how to manipulate our fate.

The runes (or staves) should be made of natural materials such as wood, stone, or bone. Traditionally, they were constructed by the caster and colored with red pigment; in some cases blood would be used but is not necessary. The goal of creating your own rune set is to develop a deep energetic connection between the runes and yourself. However, any set of runes that can be purchased will work just as well. The runes should be cast upon a white cloth. This is not a necessity, but there is something to be said about tradition.

Today, many charm casters, bone throwers, and cleromancy readers add runes to their casting kits and utilize grids, charts, and spreads to read the runes. The rune-staves should be stored in a leather or cloth pouch or wooden box large enough to mix and draw runes with the hand. Furthermore, they should be cast from horn or wood—if a wooden box is available, it will suffice to be cast from. A cup for casting lots made of natural material can also be utilized to store your runes.

The techniques for casting your runes can be personal or traditional, as you see fit. However, there should be some form of that ritualistic approach to each. As you learn and expand your practice of the runes you will find what works for you. If you are adding aspects of rune casting to further expand your cleromancy skills, you may find a technique that is more intuitive than traditional to the ways of traditional Norse rune craft. The aim of any technique is to help the reader enter into an altered state of mind required for divination.

# NORNIC RUNECAST

The following method in rune casting is known as the Nornic Runecast, in which the three Norns (Urdhr, Verdhandi, and Skuld) are used to impart knowledge of the past, present, and future. This rune-casting method, explored in much greater detail in *The Runecaster's Handbook* by Edred Thorsson, goes as follows:

**YOU WILL NEED:**

Set of runes

White cloth

Wooden cup or box (for casting)

**STEP 1**

With eyes closed, cast the runes onto the cloth randomly.

**STEP 2**

With eyes closed, choose three runes at random, placing them in a triangle following the the chart below.

Runes shown stave face up and stave face down

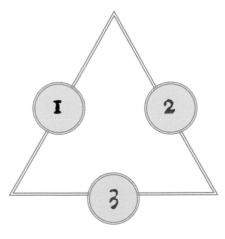

1 Urdhr    2 Verdhandi    3 Skuld

The first position, Urdhr, represents the past actions that have created or are the root of the issue and speaks of past actions that have influenced the present day. The second position, Verdhandi, reveals how past actions are now manifesting in the present moment. Lastly, the third position, held by Skuld, tells of how the future is based on what has happened in the past and what is happening in the present.

Runes, when cast, may appear face stave up (with the rune showing) or stave down, also known as bright stave and murkstave. Bright staves hold a more positive value while murkstaves foretell of a more negative aspect. It is not necessary to read the murkstave, but it would serve the caster well to learn both meanings in order to interpret fully the message being conveyed by the runes.

# CARTOMANCY

Face it, when it comes to fortune telling and divination, the first image that probably comes to mind is tarot cards, followed by a crystal ball or palmistry hand. There's a reason cards have stood out as the main calling card and symbol for psychics. It's because cards have served as a very accurate tool in the psychic's arsenal.

Cartomancy is the art of reading cards for divinatory purposes. While the very popular tarot falls under this category, usually cartomancy is restricted to using standard playing cards—the popular choice for those who practice conjure or any other magical folk practices. When playing cards took Europe by storm in the 14th century, the divinatory use for them developed shortly thereafter. The first use of playing cards for divination purposes has been attributed to the Romani people and fortune tellers during the early 15th century in France. Early playing card decks were painted by hand or with wood blocks and had sharp, crude edges and blank backs.

Despite the popularity of tarot in today's modern world, playing cards were actually the most common and preferred method of divination from the late 17th century to early 1900s. This was in part due to the accessibility of playing cards, as well as the simplicity of reading them. The difference between playing cards and the tarot is the additional 22 cards in the tarot known as the major arcana,

which hold additional occult meanings, as well as the court card known in tarot as the Page. Unlike tarot, reading with playing cards is a little more cut and dry. Cards are read individually as well as collectively, with the reader often paying attention to card coupling, matching suits, and which colors tend to dominate a layout. Cards are usually arranged in a spread, but can also be arranged within a specific board meant just for a cartomancy reading or specific question.

Another wonderful thing about cartomancy is that it is the perfect companion to a cleromancy reading. You can easily throw cards and then toss some bones on the cards for additional insight or clarification. A cartomancy deck for today's reader usually consists of the standard deck used for bridge or poker (i.e., 52 cards split into 4 suits). The deck is often is read with the Jokers, and even sometimes with the blank card found in many commercial decks. (I sometimes use this as a wild card or wish card.) In France, a 32-card deck known as a piquet deck was,

and often still is, most typically used in cartomancy readings—this deck is similar to the popular oracle deck known as the Leonormand oracle. You can create your very own piquet deck by starting with a 52-card deck and removing all of the twos through the sixes. This will leave you with only the sevens through the tens, the court cards, and the aces. According to some, a deck that is used for cartomancy should not be used for any other purpose.

Like any divinatory tool, if you're going to utilize playing cards for divination purposes, it is best to choose a deck that will only be used for readings. Some readers feel that the cards should never be touched by anyone other than their owner, however; I tend to disagree since I personally believe that you need the energy of the person you're reading for to give accurate predictions, and therefore I often let them choose their own cards after I shuffle and spread out the deck before them.

## PLAYING CARD SUITS/ TAROT EQUIVALENTS

Here is a breakdown of the suits and their divinatory meanings in cartomancy, as well as their tarot counterparts (minus the 22 major arcana cards).

**Clubs**
Rods, batons, or wands (power, communication, people, community) Fire

**Diamonds**
Coins/Pentacles (physical, tangible, sex, material matters, career) Earth

**Hearts**
Cups (emotions, love, romance) Water

**Spades**
Swords (intellect, action, obstacles) Air

While cartomancy is considered a fixed system, you will find that the interpretations and meanings given in this book may vary from other books written about cartomancy and divination with playing cards. This is because unlike the tarot, which was given occult meanings by specific occultists and published with the intention to be read in the same way universally, playing cards were attributed divinatory meanings by many different people of various ethnic groups, cultures, and folk practices from across Europe. Even the cartomancy practices of the American South are different from those in Europe. The card interpretations listed here are based on key words and the reading system of playing cards that matches those of the French-style cartomancy system, and also that of the minor arcana of the French Marseilles tarot of the late 17th century.

## THE CARDS AT A GLANCE

The following grid outlines the key words associated with the cards and is by no means meant to offer a complete description of the card. It is also important to know that the meanings of the cards will change slightly based on the position of the card, the surrounding cards, and the question that's being asked during the reading.

**Aces**
Beginnings,
a new journey.

**Twos**
Partnerships,
future planning,
conversations.

**Threes**
Growth, cycles,
new developments,
good omens.

**Fours**
Stability,
grounding,
support.

**Fives**
Swiftness, chaos,
inconvenience,
changes.

**Sixes**
Rewards harvested,
favors reciprocated,
good fortune
returned, luck.

**Sevens**
Deceit, cunning,
cruelty, theft,
misfortune.

**Eights**
Journey, progress,
transition,
movement.

**Nines**
Blessings bestowed,
very good fortune,
a wish fulfilled,
YES.

**Tens**
Completion,
an ending,
victory, full circle.

**Knights**
Strength, vigor.

**Queens**
Wisdom, cunning,
maternal, feminine,
true mastery.

**Kings**
Power, domination,
control, masculine.

# CARTOMANCY 3-CARD SPREAD

This is a great introductory spread for anyone new to cartomancy, as well as for those who don't necessarily have a specific question they'd like to ask the cards.

YOU WILL NEED:

Deck of standard playing cards

**STEP 1**
Shuffle your deck of cards thoroughly.

**STEP 2**
Spread out the cards before you face down.

**STEP 3**
Pull three cards and flip them over left to right.

**Left card: Obstacle**
The card on the left is read as your current obstacle. If the card is normally a positive card, then you would have to look and see why this is an opposing force by perhaps making it a negative.

**Center card: Card of self**
This card reveals the qualities and abilities at your current disposal that can help you overcome your obstacles and achieve your goals.

**Right card: Things to come**
The card on the right reveals what will happen in the future.

# CHAPTER SIX
# BOARDS

Boards, charts, grids, and casting cloths have been utilized alongside various divination methods such as cleromancy and dowsing for millennia. Today there are many different types of boards out there. Many have been designed for specific or niche purposes, like specifically looking at family or love. Others are very intricate boards that are able to answer almost any question one could think of. While reading without a board is possible, it does make a considerable difference when you have some formation or layout you can use alongside your reading.

The main purpose of a board during a cleromancy or pendulum reading is to have a reference of possible images, letters, numbers, and symbols that might come up when those specific elements on the board are touched. This adds more detail to a reading and helps us connect with our intuition in a deeper way. Why did the coyote tooth land on the letter A? Perhaps someone whose name begins with the letter A is gossiping about you, or A is the grade you're going to get on a test you'll be taking soon. The interpretation will vary depending on who you're reading for and if a question has been asked.

Boards can be simple or complex and vary in terms of design and detail. They can be circular, semicircular, square, or rectangular, and vary by theme. A board for health may have a list of issues, modalities, and remedies that one may use a pendulum with in order to gain additional insight into someone's health. Another board may feature key words that can only be interpreted if a pendulum targets a specific word or a bone lands on the board during the casting of a cleromancy reading.

The boards within this book are meant to help you expand your cleromancy and pendulum readings. When deciding which board to use for a reading, you should first think of the question you'd like to ask and then think of the divinatory system you'd like to use. Does the question in mind seem like it could be answered with a simple yes/no? Perhaps use a pendulum and a yes/no board. Need general guidance from a spirit guide or your higher self? You may want to throw some bones on a more detailed board. At the end of the day, the best way to utilize the boards has more to do with the answers you seek and the tools you wish to use.

# HOW TO CAST LOTS ON A BOARD

Casting lots on a board is simpler than you might think. The board serves as a map or outline, usually designed with a specific layout that can be used alongside a specific question or for general purposes.

When casting lots on a board you must first decide the focus of your reading. Are you reading with a specific question in mind? Are you looking to communicate with a spirit or deity? Perhaps you want a general reading or a weekly forecast? Knowing this information will allow you to choose which board is most appropriate for the reading you're about to undertake.

The boards best suited for casting bones are generally those that have specific sections and key words on them. This is because it allows the bones to serve as markers; when the bones land on a letter, word, or number, you can read it in accordance to which bone landed on that specific part of the board.

## Getting started

**STEP 1**
Pick a board in accordance to your question or the type of reading you have in mind.

**STEP 2**
Burn some incense or prepare any opening ritual you'd like to do before bone casting.

**STEP 3**
Think of the reading about to take place and call on any ancestors, spirit guides, or deities you may wish to have present to assist during the casting.

**STEP 4**
Shake and cast your bones onto the board.

**STEP 5**
Pay attention to the layout of the board and note where the bones land. Disregard any that fly off the board.

**STEP 6**
Read the bones in accordance with the cast that's been thrown and the messages that are revealed from the bones and the numbers, symbols, letters, or words the bones land on.

**STEP 7**
Write down anything that appears unclear, or that you may wish to look into further.

---

### THINGS TO LOOK FOR WHEN CASTING LOTS ON A BOARD

✳

Where did the bones land? Are they close together or far apart?

✳

Did any bones fly off the board? Disregard those in a reading.

✳

Are any half in the board and half out? Those might be messages from spirits.

✳

Pay attention to bones that land on messages, words, and numbers. Write them down, also noting the specific bone or curio that landed on them.

✳

Pay attention to the imagery on the board and where the bones are touching, as well as the direction the bones face.

# THE BOARDS AT A GLANCE

Below, you'll find a quick visual reference to the 20 boards featured in this book, along with
their names and page references, to make it easier to choose the right board for your session.

Bone Casting, 80

Druid Circle, 82

Greco-Roman, 84

Oracle, 86

All Seeing Eye, 88

Wheel of Fortune, 90

Serpent, 92

Medusa's Gaze, 94

Wishing Star, 96

The Seer's Eye, 98

Sun and Moon, 102

Astrological, 104

Prophetic Pendulum, 106

Venus Vibes, 110

Hecate's Weekly
Prediction Wheel, 112

Weekly Guidance
Forecast, 114

Minotaur's Maze, 116

The Sybil's Circle, 118

The Witches' Board, 120

The Fool's Journey, 122

## BOARD 1
# BONE CASTING

This board is perfect for readings that involve in-depth, open-ended questions that relate to themes such as love/relationships, finance/career, or personal issues, as well as spirit communication. The board is split into four sections. The sections closest to the querent represent the immediate future, while those further away will reveal what has yet to be. The left side of the grid usually indicates the spiritual, while the right side represents the mundane (everyday). Pay attention to the symbols and images that the bones land on, since this will add additional meaning.

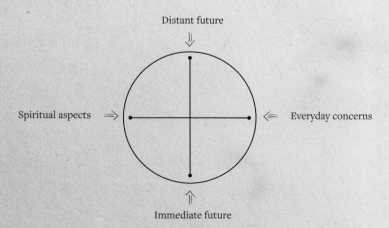

## BOARD 2
# DRUID CIRCLE

The druids were known to be the spiritual and magical folk of the Celtic peoples. They were skilled in herblore, medicine, sorcery, and, of course, divination and prophecy. This board invokes their wisdom and allows one to ask a yes/no question that may have a journey and require discovery. Are you looking to move? Perhaps you are wondering if you should change jobs or if the person you're interested in is worth pursuing romantically? These are questions the druid circle can help find the answers to.

The resolution

The issue at hand

Action to take

Contributing factors

NO

YES

Things to avoid

Your inner self

Others involved

Current energy

## BOARD 3
# GRECO-ROMAN

The Ancient Greeks and Romans relied heavily on divination, and cleromancy was one of their preferred methods. Throwing knucklebones and dice were a means by which many people during the Greco-Roman period, nobles and commoners alike, answered many of life's problems. The SATOR square is a five-line Latin palindrome that can be read in every direction: backward, forward, up, and down. It's comprised of magical words, and its symmetry only adds to its magic.

While we do not really know the original meaning or purpose behind the SATOR square, we do know that the earliest usage of it dates back to Pompeii in 62 CE. In medieval times it became known as a charm for good fortune and has since been adopted into many magical systems and found in grimoires throughout Europe. This board is perfect for when you don't have a particular question in mind, or perhaps want to name key information. Cast your bones onto the SATOR square and pay attention to the letters that the bones fall on—perhaps they can offer insight.

# BOARD 4

# ORACLE

The word oracle derives from the Latin *ōrāre*, meaning "to speak," and refers to a priest or priestess who acts as a medium for the gods and spirit realm and utters a prediction. Today, an oracle can refer to a person or tool utilized to help give prophetic insight. This board is intended to act as portal between you and the divine. Consult it when you need a more spiritual or divine outlook on a situation. Pay close attention to where the bones land and the messages that come up.

## BOARD 5

# ALL SEEING EYE

This board is designed specifically to tap into many different areas of one's life. It is perfect for when you or the person you're reading for doesn't have a specific question in mind. Each symbol on the board calls to a specific area of one's life: a book symbolizes knowledge, a ship symbolizes travel, and so on. This board can touch on all aspects of life and even reveal things that perhaps you haven't even thought of yet.

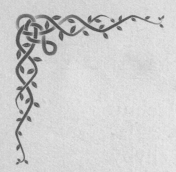

BOARD 6

# WHEEL OF FORTUNE

The wheel of fortune is unpredictable, and so, too, is this board. It allows the bones to tap on the various aspects of our life that are worth reading on, much like the spokes of a wheel. This board is best utilized without a question in mind, but it can be used with a person in mind, as a check-in. Like all the boards in this book, pay close attention to where the bones land, their placement, and the words that are next to or underneath the bones.

# BOARD 7
# SERPENT

In many cultures around the world the snake is a sign of renewal because of the need for the creature to shed its skin. The snake can both hinder and heal. In fact, the way to heal a snake bite is through the use of anti-venom; venom from the snake itself. A snake can turn on you in an instant and is unpredictable, as is life. Consult this board when you are unsure of a decision or you wish to ask a specific question. This board is perfect for use alongside a pendulum.

## BOARD 8
# MEDUSA'S GAZE

You've heard of Medusa, a monstrous woman with snakes for hair
and a face so horrid it can turn you to stone, but there's more to the
woman and myth than meets the eye. Medusa was once a beautiful
young priestess whose circumstances changed when she was personally
violated. This board appeals to the protective and prophetic aspects
of the mighty Gorgon. Allow Medusa to peer beyond the veil and help
answer the questions you seek. Will you, won't you? You can also look
at multiple facets of life and multiple yes/no questions with this grid.
Use in conjunction with a pendulum or bones.

## BOARD 9

# WISHING STAR

We all have dreams and desires, but sometimes life consumes us with the mundane, making our passions seem out of reach. The wishing star board is intended to help you commune with the divine on how you can actually achieve your dreams and desires. In this board, each part of the wishing star is separated in sections that will offer deeper insight into certain situations. Use this board in conjunction with your bones and you will find much clarity on how to navigate life so that you can truly have your wishes fulfilled.

## BOARD 10
# THE SEER'S EYE

Want a direct answer with no frills? This board is intended to get to the nitty gritty of a situation. Sometimes we just need to know if the answer is a resounding yes or no. This board should only be utilized if you're willing to heed the wisdom it offers you.

# READING THE SEER'S EYE BOARD

There are many different ways we can read with a board, just as there are many boards to consult when reading. The Seer's Eye Board is my favorite when you need a quick and definite answer. It is best used alongside bone casting or with a pendulum.

If you're using bones in your reading, the first thing you must do is think of a yes/no question. Let's say you're inquiring about a potential romantic relationship with someone. Think of that question and hold it in your mind's eye. When utilizing a board with bone casting there are many variations of tossing the bones. In this cast, because we are asking a simple yes/no, it's best just to start with one bone. Choose a bone that you find either represents you or the question in general. For example, if you have

**Sometimes we just need to know if the answer is a resounding yes or no.**

a bone that signifies relationships/romance, choose that bone. Close your eyes, think of your question and toss the bone onto the board. Pay attention to where the bone lands. What word does the bone touch? If the bone lands on NO, for example, then you would interpret the answer as no.

The Seer's Eye Board can also be used with a pendulum. Thinking of your question in your mind's eye, hover the pendulum over the eye illustration in the center of the board. Rest your elbow on a table or flat surface off the board while suspending the pendulum directly over the eye. Wait patiently and watch the pendulum swing. Pay attention to the words or phrase the pendulum swings to. Let's say that we are again asking about a potential relationship and the pendulum swings to the phrase "not at this time." This does not mean that there's no chance, but perhaps more time and effort are required to allow the relationship to grow before a romantic aspect can be looked at.

There are so many different yes/no questions that can be asked of the Seer's Eye Board, but it's very important that you ask clear questions and be specific. Also, a word of caution. Don't ask a question if you feel you won't like the answer, and always listen to the answer given and heed the warnings. You cannot utilize these methods of divination and then cast them aside because you don't like what you're told.

## BOARD 11
# SUN AND MOON

What is the obstacle in your life, and what is the blessing? What are you not seeing? The Sun and Moon board is meant to cast light on a specific situation, as well as show the obstacles or issues that stand in your way. Use with a pendulum, coin, or bones and see what challenges and victories will come your way regarding a certain situation.

# ASTROLOGICAL

Looking for insight from the celestial and planetary realms? Perhaps you wish to gain clarity on a specific person? This board is designed to flesh out the missing details with the help from the planetary houses. This board may be a bit tricky for those not used to astrology, but once you familiarize yourself with the zodiac signs, traits, and archetypes of each house, you will find that this board can help fill in the blanks and add key information during a reading. Ask about a friend, partner, or loved one. Perhaps look at the forecast of a specific life decision such as an upcoming move. Utilize with both pendulums and bones.

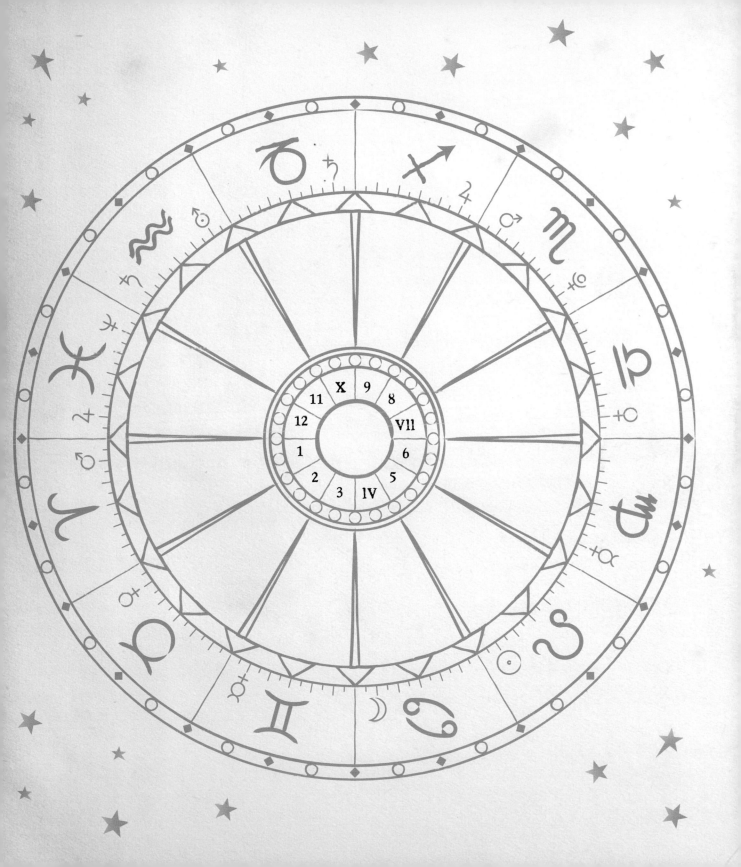

# PROPHETIC PENDULUM

This board is specifically intended to work alongside a pendulum for dowsing. This expanded board can assist with a plethora of different questions, from simple yes/no to more open-ended questions. You may also consult this board when you don't have a specific question in mind or if you'd like to communicate with a spirit guide or deity, or a deceased loved one. Letters, signs, and numbers appear on the board to help offer answers to questions. Keep in mind that the spirit realm does not communicate like we do, so answers often will be cryptic and require interpretation.

## BOARDS IN DEPTH

# READING THE PROPHETIC PENDULUM BOARD

Utilizing the pendulum as a tool in readings is actually quite trippy. To this day I often battle with the question, "Is this me moving it, or not?" Given that I've strengthened my connection to the spirit realm, I'd like to believe it is my spirit guides communicating through it, but I've always called myself the "skeptic psychic." To be completely honest, aside from spirit and séance work, I don't really utilize a pendulum. Probably because my skepticism often gets the better of me, or because I've freaked myself out by it one too many times. With that said, the pendulum board here is truly a marvelous companion to reading with a pendulum and can offer a wide range of answers to specific questions.

Let's use my friend Sarah as an example. She has been debating about whether or not she should move out of state and pursue a different career. Being a very spiritual person, her go-to method of divination is the pendulum. Now, because she and I are similar, she decides that she'd like me to consult the pendulum on her behalf. The first thing I do is perform a smoke cleansing for my pendulum by burning some dragon's blood incense. This ensures that I've cleared the pendulum of any stagnant energy that could've clung to the pendulum. Then I place my elbow firmly on the table and allow my pendulum to suspend freely over the board. I ask Sarah to ask her question aloud and she says, "Should I move out of state?" Focusing on her question, I direct the energy of the question I heard into the pendulum.

Looking at the board, I see that the pendulum is swinging toward the word YES. I hold the pendulum in my hand and prompt Sarah to ask another question, this time one that is open ended. She asks, "How soon should I move?" I once again suspend the pendulum over the board, and after a few seconds, the pendulum swings between the numbers 3 and 4. These numbers put us in a bit of suspense; is it months, days, years? Sarah asks if it's indicating months and the pendulum swings to NO. Sarah then asks if she will have job prospects out of state. Here the pendulum swings to the letters A, T, S, T. These random letters stump both of us, but she notes them in her phone. At this point we both feel that the reading has served its purpose and put things on pause. Later Sarah will inform me that she's always wanted to be an ARTIST, and while the pendulum didn't quite spell that out, it did open the door in her mind by hitting those letters.

This is just one example of the many styles and variations of things that can appear on the pendulum board.

*Make sure your questions are specific, and always write down any letters and numbers the pendulum swings over.*

You can and should always follow up with a yes/no question for additional clarification.

# BOARD 14
# VENUS VIBES

Have someone you're sweet on? Looking to gain further insight into your
relationship with a specific someone? Why not ask Venus, the Roman
goddess of love? This relationship forecast board serves as the perfect
oracle for the person you have a romantic interest in. Use this board in
conjunction with cards or bones and see what the goddess of love has to
say about your relationship or romantic partner.

Represents me in the relationship

Our strengths

An activity we should do

Past challenges

Represents my partner in the relationship

Our weaknesses

What we should focus on

Current challenges

Future challenges

An activity we should do

External influences

Represents us together

How we can better communicate

Advice from higher self

Something to consider

BOARD 15

# HECATE'S WEEKLY PREDICTION WHEEL

Hecate is the Greco-Roman goddess of witchcraft, magic, necromancy, crossroads, and the moon. As such, prophecy and divination are under her dominion. This board can be used alongside casting bones and can offer key insights into the upcoming week. Pay close attention to the planetary signs the bones land on, as that will reveal key attributes and the temperature of specific situations appearing within the week. Write down the forecast or take a picture of your throw to document for later reference throughout the week.

BOARD 16

# WEEKLY GUIDANCE FORECAST

Uncertain of what the week ahead looks like? Why not strengthen your prophetic and divinatory skills by performing a weekly forecast reading. This board allows you to perform a cleromancy throw and discover what might be awaiting you in the upcoming week. The board is divided into specific sections that will tap into certain areas of your life. Look at where on the board the bones fall and write down your findings. This is a great board for generic mini-readings.

## BOARD 17
# MINOTAUR'S MAZE

Have a situation or problem that you don't quite know how to resolve?
Just like Theseus went into the labyrinth and slew the mighty Minotaur,
you too must face a maze of your own to solve the problems that riddle
you. This board serves as the thread that will allow you to find your way
out of the problems at hand. You may cast bones or cards on this board.
Pay attention to key words and follow the wisdom revealed.

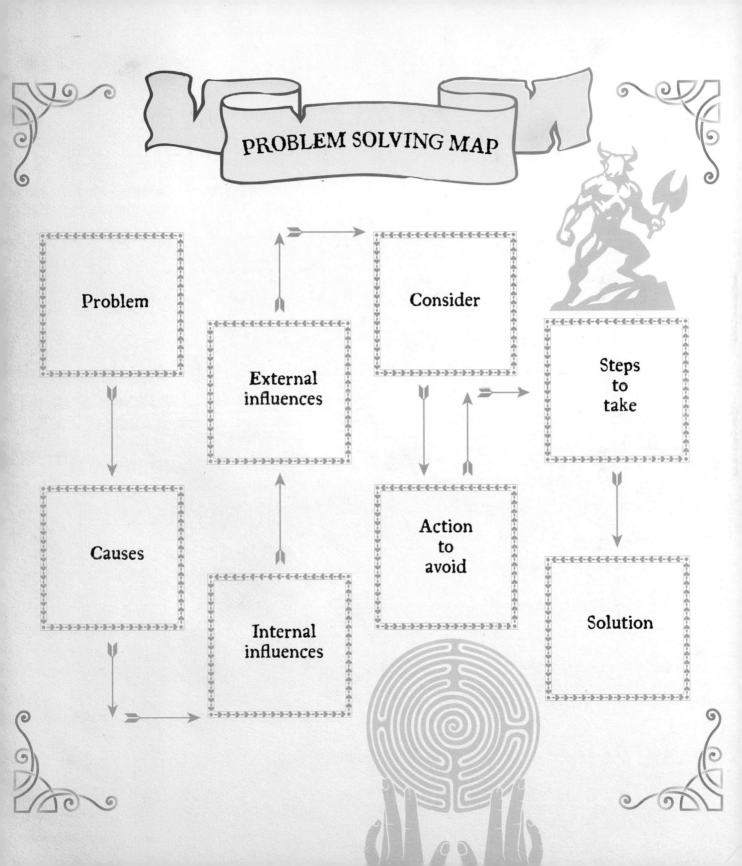

# PROBLEM SOLVING MAP

Problem

Causes

External influences

Internal influences

Consider

Action to avoid

Steps to take

Solution

## BOARD 18
# THE SYBIL'S CIRCLE

The Sybils were sacred priestesses in Ancient Greece and Rome whose main function was to serve as oracles and give prophetic wisdom. This board channels the wisdom of those ancient Sybils and is perfect to use when you do not have a specific question in mind. It can be utilized alongside casting bones as well as playing cards or tarot cards. Cast the bones onto the board to see what questions they answer or shuffle the cards and turn them over on each designated space to create a simple spread.

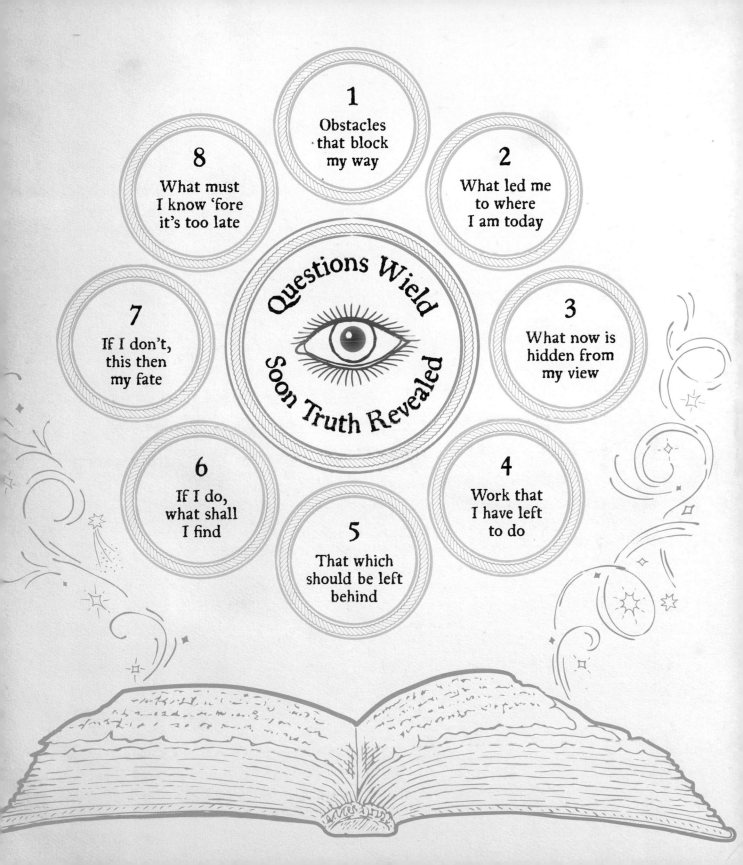

BOARD 19

# THE WITCHES' BOARD

Witches utilize the elements of earth, air, fire, water, and spirit to enhance their power. Being in contact with the elements and spirit also allows them the gift of prophecy and insight. This board taps into the witches' elemental connection to gain insight and clarity on specific situations. It is perfect for casting bones, dowsing with a pendulum, or throwing cards on top of. Pay attention to the elements that are targeted, as well as the side and placement of your spread.

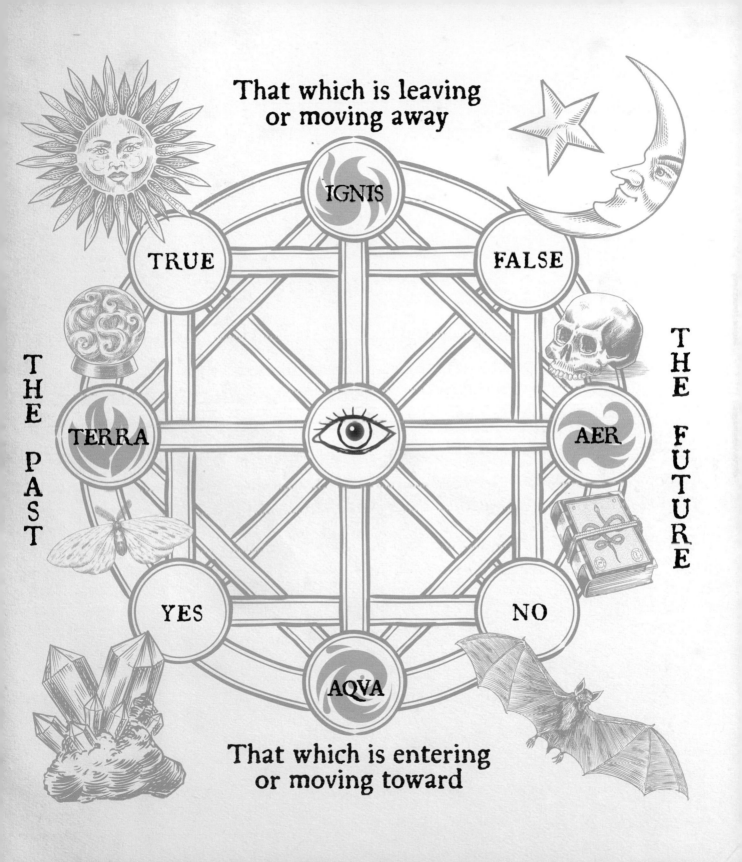

That which is leaving
or moving away

IGNIS

TRUE

FALSE

THE PAST

TERRA

AER

THE FUTURE

YES

NO

AQVA

That which is entering
or moving toward

# THE FOOL'S JOURNEY

This board's name is based on the character of The Fool, who appears in the major arcana of the tarot. It is his journey that reflects ours during a reading, and his archetype that we follow throughout the cards. This board is perfect to use when you do not have a specific question in mind, and it can be utilized alongside casting bones as well as playing cards or tarot cards. Pay attention to the tarot archetypes that the bones or cards land on and fuse the archetypes of the tarot with the cards or bones they sync with when cast on the board. You may also use a pendulum to gain insight by seeing which tarot archetypes the pendulum lands on.

# READING THE FOOL'S JOURNEY BOARD

While I love cleromancy and throwing bones, my first love and introduction to divination was through the use of tarot. The symbolism in tarot is truly magnificent and the way that the cards reflect a person's soul and psyche is magical at best. The tarot is essentially a map of a person, their book of life that is revealed to them in chapters and small sections during a reading. Each card corresponds to a certain aspect of a person's life and prompts them to make certain decisions based on the obstacles and blessings that are presented during the reading.

The first 22 cards, known as the trumps or major arcana, are the cards of deeper knowledge. These title cards reflect different archetypes that are often linked to the person being read. Each card has specific attributes and corresponds to different events. The first card in the major arcana is The Fool. In the older tarot decks such as the Tarot de Marseilles, The Fool is unnumbered and therefore can appear anywhere amongst the major arcana. The Fool, as the first archetype, is often seen as the protagonist in a story that links and connects the major arcana together. The Fool begins his journey and meets these other characters, sometimes making a cameo again as The Hanged Man, or chained up with The Devil. The Fool's Journey board is meant to be read with a pendulum, cards, or bones. For this example, we shall utilize bones.

I recently wanted to inquire about a friend I was having personal issues with and used the Fool's Journey board for additional insight on the situation. Thinking of my question and forming it in my head, I asked around, "What do I need to know about my relationship with my friend?" I picked a handful of bones from my kit and tossed them on top of the board. The bones that fell out were a rattlesnake rib bone, a coyote tooth, a gator foot, a mercury dime heads up, and a raccoon penis bone. As I stared at the board, I looked at where the bones had landed.

The rattlesnake rib bone landed right over The Empress card. Knowing that The Empress in tarot is a maternal figure, supportive and caring, plus seeing that the rattlesnake rib was covering it, I could tell that this indicated that this person was protecting their emotions, withholding how they were really feeling. I also saw that the coyote tooth had fallen right on top of The High Priestess. The coyote is a trickster and the tooth in my kit represents gossip and trickery. The High Priestess is a card of intuition and knowledge. This to me indicates that her intuition is being outweighed by gossip, and the words and influence of others. The rest of the bones jumped off the board and were therefore discarded from the reading, however the gator foot was touching the perimeter of the board pointing toward The Chariot. The gator is the apex predator and is associated with control and dominance. The Chariot is a card of victory and also, in timing, indicates things happening quickly. I deduced this to mean that if things were to be remedied between my friend and I, I would need to take initiative and act quickly.

After taking notes on my casting and cross-referencing with the cards and their meanings, I started a conversation with my friend and was able to mend things, while also finding out that people were indeed gossiping and meddling.

*Always remember to look at the individual meanings of your bones and the cards on the board, then combine the meanings to flesh out the reading.*

# INDEX

## Dedication and Special Thanks

This book is dedicated to my parents, Steven Bauer and Ingrid Anderson; my beloved grandmother, Momcat; my dearest brother, Alexander; and my fierce friends and mentors who've supported and encouraged me. And to Laurie Johnson, my mentor who taught me tarot and encouraged me to explore other divination methods, as well as witchcraft.

Special thanks to my bestie, Chad, for his contributions to the rune craft portion of this book as well as for keeping me on track with my deadlines, and to Becca Wallace for her astrology contributions and helping me create an appropriate chart to use. To Ella Whiting and the Quarto team for their patience and kindness as I conjured up this book, and to Judika Illes for her constant support and encouragement.

Lastly, I'd like to thank the seers, psychics, occultists, and mystics who were pioneers in the divination world and paved the way for us so that we may share our skills and read openly and freely for others.

## Further Reading

Here is a list of several works that not only helped me and my divinatory studies but were also referenced and utilized when conjuring up this book. I definitely suggest these titles as an addition to your personal library.

✶ *The Fortune Telling Book: The Encyclopedia of Divination and Soothsaying* by Raymond Buckland (Visible Ink Press, 2003)

✶ *Divination Conjure Style: Reading Cards, Throwing Bones, and Other Forms of Household Fortune-Telling* by Starr Casas (Weiser Books, 2019)

✶ *The Book of Séances: A Guide to Divination and Speaking to Spirits* by Claire Goodchild (Voracious, 2022)

✶ *Cartomancy in Folk Witchcraft: Playing Cards and Marseille Tarot in Divination, Magic, and Lore* by Roger J. Horne (Moon Over the Mountain Press, expanded edition, 2022)

✶ *The Element Encyclopedia of Secret Signs and Symbols* by Adele Nozedar (HarperCollins, 2009)

✶ *Greek and Roman Necromancy* by Daniel Ogden (Princeton University Press, 2004)

✶ *The Big Book of Runes and Rune Magic: How to Interpret Runes, Rune Lore, and the Art of Runecasting* by Edred Thorsson (Weiser Books, 2018)

✶ *Runecaster's Handbook: the Well of Wyrd* by Edred Thorsson (Weiser Books, 1999)

✶ *Throwing the Bones: How to Foretell the Future with Bones, Shells, and Nuts* by Catherine Yronwode (Lucky Mojo Curio Company, 2012)